THE LITTLE BOOK

of

FENG SHUI

A Room-by-Room Guide to Energize,
Organize, and Harmonize Your Space

KATINA Z. JONES

ADAMS MEDIA

New York   London   Toronto   Sydney   New Delhi

Adams Media
An Imprint of Simon & Schuster, Inc.
100 Technology Center Drive
Stoughton, MA 02072

First Adams Media hardcover edition
January 2020

ADAMS MEDIA and colophon are
trademarks of Simon & Schuster.

For information about special
discounts for bulk purchases, please
contact Simon & Schuster Special
Sales at 1-866-506-1949 or
business@simonandschuster.com.

The Simon & Schuster Speakers
Bureau can bring authors to your live
event. For more information or to
book an event contact the Simon &
Schuster Speakers Bureau at 1-866-
248-3049 or visit our website at
www.simonspeakers.com.

Interior design by Priscilla Yuen
Interior illustrations by Eric Andrews;
images © Simon & Schuster, Inc.

Manufactured in China

10 9 8 7 6 5 4 3

Library of Congress Cataloging-in-
Publication Data
Names: Jones, Katina Z., author.
Title: The little book of feng shui /
Katina Z. Jones.
Description: Avon, Massachusetts:
Adams Media, 2020.
Includes index.
Identifiers: LCCN 2019039411 |
ISBN 9781507212462 (hc) |
ISBN 9781507212479 (ebook)
Subjects: LCSH: Feng shui.
Classification: LCC BF1779.F4 J664
2020 | DDC 133.3/337--dc23
LC record available at
https://lccn.loc.gov/2019039411

ISBN 978-1-5072-1246-2
ISBN 978-1-5072-1247-9 (ebook)

Contents

Introduction

———

Feng shui is often thought of as the practice of moving furniture around to attract wealth, but it is so much more than that. Feng shui is about bringing your home and possessions into balance and harmony with the positive energy of the universe. Doing so brings you greater happiness, prosperity, and peace, generating an overall sense of well-being.

The Little Book of Feng Shui will walk you room by room through your home, workspace, and outdoor areas and demonstrate how to get rid of unnecessary clutter and arrange your belongings in ways that will allow positive energy and chi to flow through. From your living room and kitchen to your bedroom and bathroom, this book will show you how to maximize your spaces to attract the best energy possible and give you solutions for when you come across a problem that is blocking good energy from coming into your life.

This compact, practical, and easy-to-understand guide will lead you through all you need to know to enrich your home and life with the benefits of feng shui—without taking up all of your time. Feng shui can bring an intentional harmony to your home, creating a balance between nature and man-made items that allows you to receive all the positive things the universe has to offer you!

PART 1

FENG SHUI BASICS

Chapter 1

The Fundamental Feng Shui

From its literal translation, *feng shui* means "wind and water." Wind moves the invisible life force of feng shui—chi—and water retains or cultivates it. An ancient Chinese system, feng shui teaches people how to create harmony between nature and man-made structures. The belief was that this intentional harmony would ultimately balance out the world, bringing peace and prosperity to all.

A History of Feng Shui

Feng shui, or the practice of arranging possessions and surroundings so that they are in balance and harmony with the positive energy of the universe, began thousands of years ago in ancient China. Back then in southern China (a rich, fertile region filled with mountains, rivers, valleys, and farms), the art of feng shui was born out of necessity. There was a definite need among the people to determine the best and most auspicious places for their homes, altars, and burial grounds. The burial sites were particularly important to the people, since they relied heavily upon the energy of their ancestors for everything from good crops to spiritual guidance and assistance with prosperity.

To these primitive yet wise rural people, everything spiritual and ethereal had its earthly correspondent in nature—and everything in nature could be carefully "directed" to assist in the achievement of earthly goals. What were (and are) those goals? Simply put, to achieve a positive flow of energy, a balance of yin and yang, and an interaction of the five elements.

Feng shui means, literally, "wind and water." The practice of feng shui relates to the positive flow of energy through your indoor, outdoor, and spiritual surroundings. It isn't just about moving furniture around to attract wealth!

Although we are many miles and several centuries away from the original feng shui masters, we share a common belief today that external factors affect our internal landscapes, whether for good or ill.

We know that there are invisible cosmic forces that govern all things—humankind, nature, and the universe—and the main goal of feng shui is to learn to move gracefully within this flow. It's definitely not a religion, and it's not about moving some stuff out of your house so you can go get more stuff. In feng shui, it's the energy or chi that counts most, followed by good intention and personal integrity. It requires an open mind, but also one that can take an objective and honest look around at its surroundings and be ready to give up in order to receive.

Do you need to practice the principles of good feng shui in every single room of your house? No, you don't. But remember—the more you create using feng shui principles in your life, the better your overall results are likely to be.

The Feng Shui Schools

Today, there are many different methods that practitioners use to help others move their possessions and elements in the right direction. But there are only three basic schools of feng shui:

FORM SCHOOL

The Form School began in rural southern China and focuses on the lay of the land (i.e., landforms), water formations, and the topography of the land. Practitioners of this school will generally spend most of their time evaluating the lot your home is situated on and the relationship of each area of your home to the land surrounding it.

COMPASS SCHOOL

In northern China, where there just weren't as many hills, the Chinese devised a more scientific method of finding the right directions for homes, people, and possessions: They created a compass called the "luo pan." Many places of the world use this method, but because it requires the use of a compass and some mathematical prowess, many Westerners find it too difficult to use on their own. If this school is appealing to you, you should find a practitioner who is skilled in the Compass School—attempting to use the compass on your own could result in inaccurate readings or results.

BLACK HAT (OR BUDDHIST) SECT

Founded by Professor Thomas Lin Yun, the Black Hat Sect (or School) synthesizes Buddhism, Taoism, shamanism, and folk wisdom. It encourages anyone who practices feng shui, professional or novice, to rely heavily upon their intuition. The only feng shui tool a Black Hat practitioner uses is the bagua, since much emphasis is placed on intuition and intention. In the Black Hat Sect, if it feels right, it probably is—as long as there is a positive, healthy flow of chi. Black Hat also incorporates the Zen practice of meditation. This book will focus primarily on the Black Hat School.

Balancing Yin and Yang

The concept of yin and yang, the eternal opposites, is common to all schools of feng shui study and practice. But what exactly are yin and yang—and how do they work in the world of feng shui?

In their simplest sense, they represent two opposing yet complementary halves of a whole—the duality of the universe.

- "Yin" is the female energy, which is soft, nurturing, flowing, passive, and contemplative. Its direction is north, the numbers associated with it are even, and its universal correspondent is earth.

- "Yang" is the male, or aggressive, energy, which is bright, solid, and creative. Yang represents odd numbers, the southern direction, and the energy of heaven.

Together, the two symbols form a whole circle and the complete universe—but each has a dot in it of the other's energy, meaning there is some yin in yang and some yang in yin to complete the whole picture.

The yin-yang symbol is round, continuous, and complementary—both energies are needed in balanced form to create wholeness. Neither is better than the other.

The symbol of yin and yang shows that we should seek the natural balance in all things, and that all things—both natural and man-made—naturally gravitate toward this balance. The same is true in human beings, all of whom contain a little of the opposite sex's energy in them.

With yin and yang, the object is to keep the balance as well balanced as possible—to not have rooms or living spaces that are too yin or too yang. The mission of feng shui is to seek out that balance in each room so you can help yourself feel grounded or centered in your living environment.

The Five Elements

A key to understanding feng shui is learning the five elements (fire, earth, metal, water, and wood) and discovering how they relate to one another in ways that mimic nature. As in nature, there are both creative and destructive cycles, and here's the "magic formula" for each:

- **Creative cycle:** Fire creates earth, earth creates metal, metal holds water, water creates wood, and wood feeds fire.
- **Destructive cycle:** Fire melts metal, metal cuts wood, wood moves earth, earth muddies water, and water puts out fire.

The Chinese believe that the universe is heavily influenced by this positive and negative (yin-yang) interaction of the five elements. A room that uses good feng shui placement has a balanced use of each element—and is not too heavy on any one element. Too much of one element (especially a powerful one like fire) can make a room feel oppressive and can actually block the chi of the home's inhabitants.

Chi is the Westernized phonetic spelling of *qi*, the force of life that flows through objects and nature in general. Chi flows through your life and your surroundings. The goal of feng shui is to direct chi in a more positively flowing manner.

ELEMENTAL QUALITIES

On a symbolic level, the elements represent order and the influence of the universe in nature and all things, including humankind.

Here are the qualities associated with each element:

- **Fire** represents emotions and corresponds to the color red. Fire energy is pure yang—strong, assertive, and dominant. In objects for décor, real fire elements such as candles or oil lamps can be used to represent the fire element in a room—or you can use symbolic items like a red star, red fabric, or even red flowers.

- **Earth** relates to the physical plane of existence. In people, earth types are grounded, organized, and very practical in all matters. They are levelheaded and hold harmony very dear to their hearts. Earth elements that can be used in décor include soil in a potted plant, yellow and brown items, or rectangular objects like a flower box that fits on a windowsill.

- **Metal** energy pertains to mental activity and thought processes. Use metal objects like metal picture frames, lampposts, sculptures, or clocks in a room to represent this pensive energy. Symbolically, you can use round items that are silver, gold, or white in color to represent metal. Just remember that the closer the relationship of the object to its natural element, the stronger the energy of the object in your home. The more symbolic you get, the less powerful the object will be in positively affecting your home situation.

- **Water** relates to spirituality, reflection, and meditation. There is always an air of mystery with water elements. To incorporate water into your home, use clear glass vases or pitchers with fresh water, glass or clear marble stones in a dish or bowl, or anything black (since black is the symbolic color of water).

You can also add the water element to a room with a water fountain or aquarium.

- **Wood** relates to intuition and the feeling of "knowingness" inside you. Wood people are strong yet flexible, trusting their inner voice to lead them to the next project or situation safely. It is best to use real live plants in your home décor to represent wood; in feng shui, bamboo sticks especially are considered to be auspicious, or full of good luck. Anything green will symbolically create the wood element in your home.

Each of these elements is represented on the bagua (see the section called "Using the Bagua—Feng Shui's Energy Map" in this chapter). The most important thing to remember about the elements is to keep them balanced—don't worry if you don't understand it all yet. Later, this book will go room by room and give you plenty of good examples!

SENSORY CONNECTION

Also key to the principles of good feng shui is the need to balance the appeal to all of the senses. After all, the senses are considered to be the human manifestation of the five elements. But how can you accomplish a balance of these energies in your home? Here's an example of how it can work: A well-balanced living room will include items that appeal to each of the senses—a scented candle (smell); soft pillows on the sofa (touch); fresh fruit in a bowl (taste); soft music or a water fountain (sound); and an interesting, dynamic piece of artwork hanging on one of the walls (sight).

Every room of the house can use this kind of attention to achieve or maintain its balance of the senses. Don't be afraid to think a little unconventionally too—you can incorporate taste into your bathroom by mixing up a fresh fruit smoothie to sip on during a bath.

Using the Bagua— Feng Shui's Energy Map

If feng shui is a way of life, then the bagua is the road map for getting to all the great places you want to be in life. Each of your endeavors is represented in a corner of the octagon—and each corner also has its corresponding colors, elements, and energy.

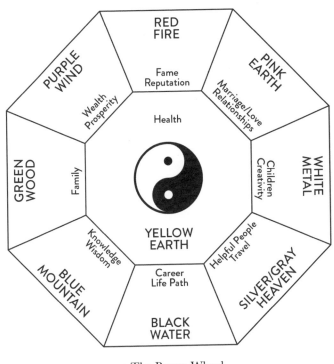

RED FIRE

PURPLE WIND

PINK EARTH

Fame Reputation

Wealth Prosperity

Marriage/Love Relationships

Health

GREEN WOOD

Family

Children Creativity

WHITE METAL

Knowledge Wisdom

YELLOW EARTH

Helpful People Travel

BLUE MOUNTAIN

Career Life Path

SILVER/GRAY HEAVEN

BLACK WATER

▲ The Bagua Wheel

Used correctly, the bagua helps you determine the preferred locations for all of your possessions—and ancient Chinese wisdom holds the belief that when you place items carefully and with intention, you clear away the blockages of energy that can hold you back from success. In other words, it's how you place your possessions that determines how well you do in life.

THE TOOL

Simply translated, *bagua* means "eight-sided figure" or "octagon." It comes from a book of ancient Chinese wisdom called the *I Ching*, or the "Book of Changes." The "Book of Changes" is a method of divination that contains insightful and profound teachings in the form of trigrams, which are symbols pertaining to business, life, and the ways of nature and the universe. The *I Ching* reveals the flow of nature as perfect balance (yin-yang) and harmony.

Each area of the bagua has a connection with the main aspects of your life: career, helpful people/travel (who assist in creating opportunities and good luck), children/creativity, relationships/marriage, fame/reputation, wealth/abundance, family/community/ancestors, knowledge/self-cultivation, and health/well-being. In feng shui, all of these "channels" are affected by both positive and negative (or blocked) energies; the goal is to keep the energies as positive and flowing as possible.

As a tool, the bagua is placed at the entrance of each location so that each area of your home or business has meaning. For example, one area represents wealth, and another represents relationships. As these sections of your home or workspace represent areas of your life, you have the potential to transform your life situation when you activate them in alignment with your clearly stated intention.

THE SECTIONS

To use the bagua, you need to place it (either physically or using your visualization ability) over the main entrance to your home with the career side aligned with the front wall. The area of career is always at the front of the location; this means that your front door is usually in knowledge, career, or helpful people.

- **Career** represents how you serve community and family. This part of the bagua demonstrates your expression in the world of work, whether as an employee, entrepreneur, or volunteer.

- **Helpful people/travel** represents teachers, mentors, helpers in life, friends, angels (as spiritual "helpers"), and opportunities brought through travel or chance meetings. It is sometimes called the "Gate of Heaven" and is the method by which luck comes into your life.

- **Children/creativity** represents all children and the incubation-like process of creativity. The creative process is key to your personal, spiritual, and psychological growth—and is absolutely critical to your career success if you are a writer, artist, or creative type.

- **Marriage/love/relationships** represents the important relationships (including marriage) of the inhabitants of the house. For a business, it represents the partners involved in running the business. The relationships corner is where you'll want to support a present relationship or conjure a new one by placing things in pairs.

- **Fame** represents reputation, image, and the way others see us in the world. Our ability to generate fame and success in business and in life depends heavily on the integrity of our intentions.

- **Wealth/abundance** represents our ability to earn, keep, and grow money. But it can also represent abundance in all things, not just the material.

- **Family/community/ancestors** represents a loving, supporting family well rooted in ancestry. The family area also supports your interaction with your community of friends with whom you gather and may share interests. If the location is an office, it supports a community atmosphere and people working in harmony.

- **Knowledge/self-cultivation** represents wisdom and the ability to acquire new knowledge. The knowledge area also supports a total path of self-knowledge and spiritual awareness.

- **Health** is in the center of the bagua and the center or "heart" of your house. It represents the individual and collective health of all living beings—including pets and plants—in a building such as your home.

Place the bagua over geographic areas in your house (either over your whole floor plan or just room by room), then look at its corresponding life endeavor. As a map of sorts, the bagua will help you determine the most auspicious locations and décor to help you achieve your life's goals. Remember, you don't have to use feng shui in every single room, but the more attention and mindfulness you give to each part of your surroundings, the better the results will be.

Changing Your Home's Energy

Before you begin the process of changing your home's energy, it's important to think about your home in its current state. What does your home say about you? If you try to view your home through the eyes of a stranger, considering the arrangement of each room, the amount of clutter or the lack thereof, the colors, the textures, the scents, and sights, what do you think your home reveals? For example:

- How much clutter is in each room of your house? Is the clutter reflective of your personality? If clutter truly reflects who you are, don't stress about it. But if you feel embarrassed by it or, worse, constrained—or if it prevents your living comfortably, keeps you awake at night, or blocks you from thinking clearly or creatively—then you should definitely take steps to eliminate the clutter and allow the chi to flow freely.

- Conversely, are your rooms too sparse? Are the walls white and bare, the furniture sterile, the space too pristine? Are guests afraid to sit or move about freely in the room or rooms for fear of making a mess or disturbing the arrangement in some way? Do you cover your furniture with plastic or rush to place coasters under every cup and glass? In other words, are you projecting unfriendliness and a "keep out" mentality to others? This is fine if you truly do not want guests showing up on your doorstep. However, if you are having trouble attracting friends to your home or keeping them there long once they arrive, it could be because the starkness of your décor or the sparseness of your furnishings is making them feel unwelcome.

- Is your home completely open to your children, or have you relegated their toys, books, and other possessions to only a room or two? Is there anything at all that is welcoming or comforting to children in the living room, the dining room, the patio, or the den? Allowing them even a little space throughout the house and a place for them to play in most, if not all, of the rooms gives children the comfort of knowing that the home is theirs too. Providing child-sized furniture and allowing a few toys in even the neatest and most sophisticated of rooms tells others that there is room in your life and your heart for something much more important than material possessions—your children.

- Is your home open, airy, and filled with light, or packed with possessions, closed, and dark? Are the colors rich and vibrant in the rooms where you spend your waking hours, and soft and relaxing in the rooms where you sleep or unwind? Can chi move easily through your rooms and hallways? Do you demonstrate awareness of the bagua in how your furnishings are arranged? Can the flow of energy in your home be improved by making minor adjustments in one or more rooms, or even in the yard or garden?

Work on one room or area of your house at a time. Do not try to feng shui your whole house in one weekend—it takes plenty of reflective time to consider your actions and to determine the changes that will feel best.

AN ENERGY AUDIT

When you first embark on your feng shui journey, it's a good idea to conduct an "energy audit" to determine areas of clear and blocked chi. Here's a quick list for assessing the chi in and around your home:

- Is the path to your front door open, curved, and inviting? Do you use your front door to enter your home, or is a side door favored? In good feng shui, your doorway should be clear and unencumbered. Too much clutter (even in the form of too much foliage) can block good energy from reaching your door.

- Are staircases easy to access—but not in direct line with doorways? Does your front door open to a staircase that goes up or down? Chi comes in through your front door and should be able to move through your house slowly for maximum benefit to all living in the home. If your staircase is in direct line with the front door, the chi rushes up the stairs and back out of the house—especially if there is a small window at the top of the staircase. Hang a crystal to slow down the chi.

- In your living room, does the air feel stagnant? That's a good sign that the energy in the room is blocked. Open some windows or use a ceiling fan to circulate the chi in the room—and bring some life back to the living room.

- Do the hallways seem open and airy? Are there piles of clutter stacked in a hallway (i.e., waiting for a move to storage that never seems to happen)?

Once you become aware of the principles of feng shui, you will see that it is not difficult to change aspects of your home and property in order to improve energy flow and open up your life to the positive results that will follow!

START WITH A CLEAN SPACE AND ADD INTENTION

In order to change your home's energy, it's important to begin with a space clearing. If weather permits, open windows to get the chi moving. Physically clean the space you will be working in. Dirt and dust symbolize stagnant chi—and that must always be cleared first!

Light a candle (pure aromatherapy type), diffuse pure essential oils, burn incense, or use a smudge stick (a tightly wrapped bundle of herbs and wood). Just be sure that whatever you use is in its purest form. Unfortunately, there are a lot of products on the market today that claim to be pure aromatherapy that are, in fact, full of artificial fillers and additives.

Play some music. A wonderful drumming or chanting song would be great, but use what you love. It doesn't have to be meditation music to speak to you.

Now you're ready for step two: intention. What is your aim, or the focus of what you most want to achieve in each area of the bagua (i.e., your life)? For instance, perhaps your intention is to attract more money. Remember your intention as you're placing the appropriate enhancement or cure (covered in the next section) in a particular sector. For example, a small water fountain in your wealth corner, with a lucky money frog placed inside, may help you attract more money.

Keep your intention clearly in your mind. Open your heart to your highest good. Embrace the possibilities, and most importantly, trust your process.

Always begin with a close look at your intentions. What do you want to accomplish? What are your goals, and which are most important to you right now? What action are you preparing yourself to take?

The next step, the house blessing, involves reinforcing all that you have done. This is the part where you meditate and offer blessings or thanks to the universe through a process called "The Three Secrets":

1 Mudra (hand gesture) is often the position of prayer, with both palms together, fingers pointing up. Hold your hands to your heart.

2 Mantra (prayer) is the prayer or blessing you are most comfortable with. It could be as simple as "Thy will be done," or maybe a simple prayer you've written on your own. Whatever

the case, recite it nine times. Nine is an auspicious number in feng shui.

3 Visualize your specific intention. As you are reciting your mantra and holding your hands in the mudra position, hold your intention in your mind's eye the entire time, as though it has already been accomplished. Use affirmative statements along with this visualization (i.e., "I have already created space for love in my life," or "I am surrounded by a loving family.").

Chances are, you'll feel uplifted and ready to take on the world when you're finished with these steps. But don't forget the last step of the whole process: Let go of the outcome—and trust the universe to do its work!

ADDING THE EIGHT REMEDIES OR CURES

Adding remedies to a specific area where the chi seems to be blocked is the best way to open up the energy to its greatest good. In feng shui, there are eight basic remedies or cures:

1 **Light** This includes lighting, mirrors, candles, and reflective surfaces.

2 **Sound** Use wind chimes, bells, metal mobiles, and hollow bamboo flutes. Anything that sounds harmonious (such as music or chanting) can also work well as a cure.

3 **Color** Red and black in particular can be used to stimulate the flow of chi.

4 **Life** Living objects, such as pets or plants, can also get the chi moving in your home or surroundings.

5 **Movement** Flags, ribbons, banners, fountains, wind chimes, weather vanes, or hanging crystals are cures associated with movement.

6 **Stillness** When chi moves too quickly, you need to slow it down with still objects such as statues or large rocks.

7 **Mechanical/electrical** This can mean machinery, but be careful that your electrical items don't overstimulate the chi. Too much energy defeats the purpose of a cure.

8 **Straight lines** Best here to use scrolls, swords, flutes, bamboo sticks, and fans.

Harness the subtle power of feng shui and its cures to move yourself in the right spiritual direction. Your feng shui mantra should be: Trust the universe. Trust your intuition. Let go of the outcome. Give thanks for all that is.

Learn to "mindfully move" the items in your environment that are creating obstacles in your life. Obstacles are not only physical items such as a couch, table, or computer, but also the mental clutter that keeps you from practicing mindfulness and holds you back from achieving your greatest potential in life.

Remember the universal law of attraction: What you put out into the universe is what you will get back. Want greater abundance in all things? Your own positive attitude is the real starting point. Clear your own negative energy first!

Chapter 2

The Art of Decluttering

It starts out rather innocently—a few things that you bought to decorate your home (or yourself)— just a few "nice things" that you couldn't pass up. Then a pattern begins—a few more bargains you couldn't refuse, a closet filled with clothes you no longer wear, an attic filled with things you don't need... Getting rid of this clutter is actually an easy thing to do—all it takes is a new perspective; a new way of taking a hard look at yourself and honestly assessing what you truly need in life.

Live a Simpler Life

The Chinese are right when they say that a cluttered house is a cluttered mind. Chinese tradition says that the more things you own, the more problems you will have in life. Think about it: When you were younger and had basically nothing, wasn't life simpler? We all seek a simpler life, yet many of us still have basements, attics, and family rooms filled with clutter.

Keeping things that are broken, useless, or obsolete is not practicing good feng shui. In good feng shui, everything you own should provide some kind of service to you—otherwise, you will become a slave to it. Functionality is key, even if the only function is to bring you joy.

The need for many things can easily go from just a bad habit to a fixation that is difficult to get over. It seems unavoidable—every day, people are inundated with more and more opportunities to buy things that will supposedly enhance their lives. The overwhelming accumulation of stuff just seems to happen, but the reality is that you have much more control over your excesses than you think. Western culture has placed such an emphasis on materialism that people actually believe they need more than they do.

Every day, it becomes harder and harder to simply accept life as it is right now, at this moment...and to back down from the infinite opportunities to "improve" it. Practice saying no to things for one day, and you'll see what conscious effort it requires!

What Clutter *Really* Means

Feng shui author Karen Kingston says the process of clearing clutter in your home environment is actually the process of releasing, of letting go emotionally. When you begin to clear the clutter in your home, you also begin to release old attachments to things that no longer serve you or bring you joy.

For instance, you might be keeping an old pair of tennis shoes that you wore on a favorite date. But as the relationship ultimately didn't work out, you are now hanging on to something that is no longer part of your life. Such tendencies can possibly hold you back from a rewarding new relationship, since, psychologically speaking, you are holding on to the past.

When you begin to clear away years' worth of clutter from your attic, you may be amazed by how much stuff from your past has been holding you back from your future. Since the attic represents higher goals or aspirations, it's no wonder you may feel like you haven't achieved all you were capable of in life. That's what good feng shui does, though—it forces you to start making conscious decisions based on your true intentions and the usefulness of items.

FEAR AND HOARDING

Don't underestimate the power of fear. As you walk through piles of old clothes, record albums, books, and knickknacks, you may ask yourself why you've been keeping all of these things for so long. Did you expect to use them again one day? Not likely. Instead, you probably hadn't felt ready to relinquish your past due to your uncertainty regarding your future.

Between changing jobs, repeated moves, or various stages of marriage, the possibility of not having enough to survive is a very real concern. Individuals in a state of continual change often take comfort in emotional hoarding, collecting things to pacify a soul that is yearning for love, for the kind of satisfaction that money can't buy. Often, they don't realize what they are doing until they have so much stuff in their homes that they can hardly breathe! Of course, if you can't breathe, neither can the chi. For good feng shui in your home, you must take a good hard look at yourself and your needs—and purge the items that no longer serve you.

The best litmus test for elimination of clutter is to look at each item and ask yourself, "When was the last time I used this?" If it was more than a year ago, it's probably not an essential item in your life—it might be of better use to someone else.

Incorporating feng shui into your lifestyle and mind-set is an ongoing process. It may be years before you realize that you are happy, secure, and certain. Continually evaluate where you are and what you need. You will know when it is definitely time for a major purging, both physically and psychologically—and what a fabulous feeling it will be to finally liberate yourself from your fears or failures of the past!

As you take a deeper look into the psychological ties you've had to the past, don't forget to check out the other clutter traps in your home. Think about clutter in the garage, in the basement, in the hall closet, and even in your car! Looking more deeply at the situation, what can you learn about your clutter patterns? Lots of interesting things. For instance, the clutter in your basement symbolizes some uneasiness in your family situation, since the basement in feng shui is symbolic of family and strong foundations.

Clutter in the garage can signify an outward manifestation of a psychological difficulty in leaving your house every day—or in coming home. If you block yourself out of your garage with clutter, you might ask yourself what it is you are having difficulty returning to in your home life. Conversely, if you are a real homebody and barricade yourself into your garage with clutter, maybe it's time to consider starting a home-based business so you can spend more time at home—in a healthier manner.

The key to dealing with clutter is to be able to take these kinds of hard looks at yourself, your needs, and your motivations in order to find out why you are keeping what you are keeping. Once you understand your motivations, you can eliminate the clutter for good—and greatly improve your inner sense of well-being in the meantime!

PROSPERITY AND ABUNDANCE

A central aspect to the study of feng shui, and metaphysics in general, is the concept of continual abundance. In prosperity consciousness (as it is also called), the more you give, the more you are open to receive. There is no such thing as "I may need it someday," because as soon as you give something away, you create a space for whatever is new and necessary at the moment. If you give in to the worry about never having enough, you will create a life in which you never have enough.

Instead, reframe your thinking to accept yourself where you are now in your life. You will always be prosperous, because you will attract positive abundance. It's such a simple concept, yet difficult for most to master without consistent (and committed) practice. It may take several years to look at yourself, and your life, from this perspective on a regular basis!

One of the basic laws of metaphysics is that what you put out to the universe is what you will receive back. So, if you tell the universe that you are poor and unhealthy, that is the life you will create for yourself, just by your own limiting mind-set.

> Provide clear passageways to the heart of each room...
> You don't want to trip your way through your house, as symbolically this will represent a struggle through life.
> Remember: If you're stuck, the chi will be too!

Sell or Donate

Having a garage sale is a great (and auspicious) way to begin your journey into the world of feng shui. By selling off excess clutter of your own and your family's, you not only free up your living space, you also fill it with good chi and a few extra dollars.

If you decide to hold a garage sale, be sure to price everything to go. Assign low prices so that you are sure to get rid of most of your stuff in one day. Then use the power of feng shui to position your soon-to-be-former belongings to sell.

BRING OUT THE BAGUA

Group like items together, then place them on tables that are slanted a little in order to activate the flow of energy around them. You want these items to radiate their energy to bargain hunters—not get lost in a huge pile of stagnant energy that is blocked by tables crammed together!

Place your most valuable items for sale on a table in your wealth corner—in the rear left corner of the bagua—right near your checkout table, if you want. The highest-priced items should be in the wealth corner to attract their best buyers.

You will greatly increase the profitability of your garage sale if you follow the bagua octagon in the placement of the items you're offering for sale. For instance, place old photo frames in your family corner (on the middle left or east side of the bagua, beneath the wealth corner) to attract shoppers who might want these photo frames to house pictures of their loved ones. For added impact, slip in a picture of a family from a magazine.

Books, DVDs, and old bookshelves should be placed on a table or shelf in the knowledge corner of your "Good Chi" bagua, just below the family section. Line the middle entrance of your driveway with old office furniture, equipment, or accessories, since this is the career corner. It also has the corresponding elements of water and ancestral energy, so things that pertain to those elements can also be included in this area of the garage sale.

Often people attempt to live their lives backward. They try to have more things, or more money, in order to do more of what they want, so that they will be happier. The way it actually works is the reverse. You must first be who you really are, then do what you need to do in order to have what you want.
—MARGARET YOUNG

To the right of your career entrance is the helpful people corner of your garage sale bagua. The elements that correspond to this corner are the heavens and travel, so here is where you might display old suitcases, photos, or posters of faraway places. You might also include any religious objects such as statues or icons.

The children's department of your garage sale should be located in the west corner of this bagua, just up from the helpful people corner. This is where you will offer all the toys your kids no longer play with and the clothes they no longer wear. In most garage sales, these are the items that get sold and resold the most! Since the corresponding element to this area of the bagua is metal, you can also include metal items such as bicycles, candlesticks, and kitchen gadgets.

Old wedding gifts you didn't use would be a good fit in the marriage/relationships corner. This area of the bagua is in the rear right, between the children's area and the fame corner. You can also put pottery and earth-related items in this section, since the corresponding element is earth. Pictures of landscapes can be placed on the ground, leaning on the tables that hold the pottery and other earth-related items.

The fame corner, which will be dead center in the south corner of your bagua, is the ideal place to sell anything that elevates the attractiveness of the individual (with the potential to bring fame and fortune). Remember those designer jeans you bought? Hang them up here with an enticing price tag. How about the exercise equipment you bought from TV? Dust it off and move it to this corner for your garage sale. And don't forget that the element that corresponds to fame is fire—making this an ideal corner to feature candles, mirrors, and fireplace tools.

USEFUL TO THE END

All of these tips may make you tired at the thought of having a garage sale. You might think you're going to a lot of extra trouble to attractively position stuff you are looking to dump anyway. But keep in mind that your possessions can serve you even as they depart your company. In other words, let your things bring you good fortune in the form of positive money energy while they are leaving your home to offer new life to another's home.

Accept the fact that you were not even using many of these items in the first place. Remember that the goal is to give up the things that no longer bring you happiness or represent who you are now, at this moment. Take a deep breath; then let go of this old, stagnant energy!

Of course, not everything will sell at your garage sale. Whatever doesn't sell you must remain committed to clearing, so remember to put those items in a small pile and call the donation truck for the charity of your choice immediately after your sale is over. There should be nothing—seriously, nothing—left once you're finished with a feng shui clearing like this one. Do not hang on to leftovers for your next garage sale—there will always be plenty of new stuff to let go of by then!

Manage Other Kinds of Clutter

Okay, so you've cleared the unnecessary clutter in your attic, garage, and basement. So in theory, you should now be ready to apply the principles of feng shui to your home, correct?

Maybe not. There are other kinds of clutter besides physical clutter—and though they are not as obvious, they can create obstacles in your life nonetheless.

- **Time clutter** occurs when you fill up your schedule with too many commitments, and then have too little time left over for your family or social life. You should always leave "open" time to allow for new opportunity, learning, or growth through experiences.

- **Mind clutter** happens when you allow your brain to fill with thoughts, worries, and concerns about the future. To alleviate this kind of clutter, you should consider journaling. Writing down your thoughts is a positive, healthy way to get worries and other forms of mental clutter out of your mind and into a safe, directed place.

- **Electronic clutter** is another insidious form of clutter that can block chi. Think about it: At this moment, you probably have undeleted voice mail, emails, and texts, or a hard drive you haven't backed up in years. Are you paying cloud storage fees for things you literally never look at? Why? You should clear as much as you can in your virtual world on a daily basis. You always want as much of your chi to be as open and flowing as possible.

- **Food clutter** is always worth a second look. If you are consuming more than your body needs, or keeping more food than you or your family will ever eat, you are exhibiting traits of a food hoarder. Constantly throwing away uneaten food that has spoiled is another sign.

If journaling seems like it might take too much time, try a "Thoughts and Worries" jar with little slips of paper containing your concerns. What you're doing, of course, is giving your anxiety clutter another place to live.

Clear the Energy of Your Home

The most important thing about clearing clutter of all kinds is to recognize that it is necessary in order to wipe your energy slate clean, so to speak. You want to start rearranging your home and surroundings in the most positive, unaffected way possible—and clutter blocks any and all good energy from flowing positively through your personal environment.

Once you've eliminated the clutter from your life, you are ready to remove stagnant, unhealthy chi from your surroundings. There are many ways to do this effectively.

A note of caution: If you're not feeling well or not in a positive mood, don't do your space clearing just yet. Wait until you feel better so that you can offer the best of your energies to the task.

Some people begin the process of space clearing with a fresh stick of lavender incense, although many feng shui practitioners use a smudge stick to do the same thing. Choose whichever better suits your mood. Lighting the incense and holding it in your hand, walk through every room in the house to send out the negative energy and welcome the positive into your environment. You may choose to say a little invocation, or prayer, to accomplish this, for example: "Negative energy, be on your way. Positive energy, begin flowing today." You can create one that works for you—there are no hard-and-fast rules, except being mindful of the purpose of this exercise.

Begin with a clean living space and body, and with clear intentions. What do you want to clear away, and what do you want to positively attract with new energy? Be clear about these things before beginning, and you'll have a better result.

Some experts think you should only do a space clearing in complete silence, but you may prefer to use some soft background music, especially if it complements your intention. Finding music that speaks to—and encourages—your goal is a powerful experience. Just remember to think about your intention, about what you want to achieve. Be mindful of your choices so they serve you or your purpose.

In terms of aromas, you can use incense, or you can light scented candles and sprinkle some mineral sea salt (a universally recognized purifier, much like baking soda) in trouble areas where the chi has been blocked. Consider using a little sea salt in your attic (or your previously identified clutter trap), around the toilet (for good pipe clearing), and in the doorway, since so many energies travel to and from there. If you find yourself falling into old traps and habits, use your trouble spot (or energy audit) checklist (Chapter 1) to determine which areas might need a little sprinkle of sea salt to clear unwanted or stale energy.

One final suggestion as you clear space in your now clutter-free domicile: Place a statue of an angel or a Buddha in the helpful people corner of each room in which you perform a space clearing ceremony. This will give you added protection—and enhance the positive chi in each room as you bless and move forward!

Space clearing will be most effective if you do it on a regular basis, such as when each new season arrives or whenever you've made any kind of change in your life. Be sure to bless the change, your space, and all who enter it from that moment forward.

PART 2

FENG SHUI IN YOUR LIFE

Chapter 3

Doorways and Entrances

In feng shui, your front door is many important things: It is the "mouth of chi" and the gateway of energy as it enters your home, but it is also the window to your world, the passage through which all others see you.

Creating a Positive Front Door

Making a good first impression is important in feng shui—but in feng shui, it's not about seeking to impress others as much as it is about mindfully projecting the picture of yourself that you want the world to see. You control how others perceive you—and if your front door is a mess of overgrown shrubbery, piles of junk, and a rusty old mailbox, others will perceive you as an unhappy, overwhelmed person whose decision-making skills are not the best.

Make sure that all the elements are represented by shape, color, or actual element in your entrance. Ensure that the shrubs are cut back, leaving a clear walkway. You want a meandering path leading to your front door; this avoids what is called "rushing chi" that flows too fast through your home.

When you mindfully project a positive image of yourself to the world around you, your front door radiates warmth, abundance, peace, and togetherness. It exudes a feeling of welcome energy while it attracts new possibilities, since it also represents new opportunities to attract abundance and prosperity to yourself and your family. It is the conduit through which chi can enter and spread its healthy qualities throughout your home and its immediate surroundings.

THE IMPORTANCE OF YOUR FRONT DOOR

The quality of chi in a house is directly related to its ability to flow in freely through your front door. This is why your door's feng shui "name" is "the mouth of chi," because it feeds chi throughout your home. Simply put, it's the only way for the good chi and all its wonderful energy to enter your home and enrich your life.

Metaphysically speaking, your door is a major center of attraction in your home. It's symbolic of all that you wish to attract or let into your life simply by opening the door. Give lots of thought to how you treat opportunity if and when it does come knocking at your door. Create an inviting doorway that attracts what you most want by sending out the appropriate message to the universe. If you want a new love relationship, place a wreath with a pink ribbon on it on your front door, and be sure to plant shrubs or trees in pairs by your doorstep. If you want wealth to start pouring in, put a penny under your welcome mat to send out the message that money is welcome here.

In many ways, your doorway is the window into your soul. If passersby see clutter around your doorway, or a view obscured by large trees or fences, what is the message to them? A clear, inviting doorway means a happy, cheerful, and open spirit dwells within your home.

SETTING THE STAGE

First of all, make sure your doorway is open and clutter-free. You don't want opportunity to trip and fall over your stuff—that would be bad feng shui, of course. Keep the door freshly painted, clean, and free of debris, and you'll open the path for greater things in your life. If the front door is anything less than clear and clean, you'll always feel like opportunity is passing you by.

Keeping your doorway clear serves another good purpose aimed at helping you reach your goals: It allows people and new opportunities to find you in the easiest, clearest way possible.

If you don't often use the front door of your home, make it crystal clear which door you intend for others to use. However, if you want new opportunities to come to you, it is strongly advised in feng shui practice for you to go in and out of your front door every once in a while to strengthen your intention.

Be sure that all near your front door is in working order. Lights should be working, hinges should not squeak, and the doorbell should ring in a way that pleases you and your visitors. If you don't have a doorbell, you can improvise by hanging a small bell on the doorknob or a wind chime near the front door. The important thing is to have a pleasant way of being notified when opportunity presents itself.

If your front door is how you project your image to the world, what color should your door be? Red front doors work best; the Chinese believe that red holds the most power and energy, making it most auspicious for a door that projects power and authority. Show your strength!

What if red just isn't your favorite color for a front door?
You can use variations of the color—anything from
burgundy to purple or even a lovely shade of mauve.
You may lean toward a deep, mauve-ish purple for your front
door if red just seems a bit too forward for your personality.
Purple is still a color of power, and it has greater
significance when it comes to wealth.

The color of your door should stand out from the other colors of your home's exterior. This draws even more energy to your front door, since it can then become the focus of your entire entranceway.

MAKING AN ENTRANCE

Once you open the door, note whether it opens nice and wide. You'll want it to so your opportunities have the most room to enter your home. If your door is too tight, you might discover that your opportunities are also limited. If it is safe to do so, keep your door wide open during the day to allow the maximum amount of light to come in, and also to signify to the world that you're ready for new and wonderful things to happen!

If your door opens inside to a straight path leading back out of the house via a back door, you have the feng shui challenge of rushing chi to contend with, so create a few boundaries along that path to slow down the energy and allow your opportunities to linger a spell. You can place a small water fountain near the front door, or perhaps a pillar with a plant on it in the hallway. If it is big enough to divert your eye's attention, it's big enough to slow down the chi. You can also use a screen or a wind chime to slow down the energy.

Another common problem with respect to the front door is the issue of a bathroom on the second floor directly above the front door. Although this is not favorable, because it puts you in the position of "flushing" opportunities back out the front door, it can be corrected by hanging a mirror on the ceiling of the entranceway below. This symbolically pushes the energy that comes in through the front door back down into the room—and keeps the flushing of the upstairs toilet from interfering with the good chi below!

If the front door creates issues with clutter for you due to daily "disturbances" such as mail, boots, coats, and the like, you can keep a good handle on the clutter by creating a designated space for such items. Ideally, you'll have a closet nearby for the clothing-related items; then all you need is a small desk or wall basket for your incoming mail. But you should keep it there only until you sort it accordingly—no month-old bills allowed—because this represents unmade decisions, which is also stagnant chi.

Improving Your Pathways

The path to your front door can be made of many materials, including wood, stone, or brick. The important consideration in feng shui, however, is the configuration. Your walk should be designed for its representation of a meandering stream. In other words, rather than having a pathway in a straight line that "beats a path" to your front door, you'll ideally want one that slows down rushing chi and allows visitors to stop and smell the roses a bit.

Some feng shui practitioners warn against roses on your path due to their thorny nature, although you may think of them as good yin-yang because of their soft petals and prickly thorns.

You could have small bushes, shrubbery, pachysandra, or even delicate flowers such as geraniums or violets welcoming visitors to your home. Just be sure to keep the flora healthy and well tended.

Whatever plant you choose to adorn your walkway, know that, aside from pure aesthetics and beauty, it will serve the purpose of slowing down the chi even more along the winding path. It will also represent your intentions, just as the seeds of your thoughts do. Whether you are planting red California poppies for fame and recognition or marigolds for better health, planting specific flora can help you stay focused on your life's goals—and can help you to literally grow your intentions from seed to reality.

A free-flowing path to your front door is good, positive use of chi. If your path isn't a winding one, consider arranging rocks around it in a more meandering pattern to slow down the chi; a straight path speeds the flow of energy (chi) right to your front door in an unhealthy manner.

Consider the house that has the inauspicious configuration of the straight-line path leading to its front door, further complicated by the fact that a busy street dead-ends right at the beginning of it! If you happen to have a straight path leading to your door, rather than tear it out and replace it with a winding one, you could simply plant more bushes or shrubs—and position them in a meandering, flowing path around the straight line of the actual walkway. It's a simple way to enhance the feeling of the meditative, winding path to your door. You could also plant a tree or, better yet, a line of pine trees as a natural barrier in the front yard to block some of the energy from rushing to your door.

In feng shui, no particular positioning is inherently bad—just challenging. You might have a very short front walk but a long driveway, and that's all right because you can connect the two by positioning rocks in a faux path that connects and makes for a much longer and auspiciously winding path to the front door. Challenging doesn't mean impossible!

What if you live in an older neighborhood that features very well-planned, straight paths to your door? Is this rushing chi? Certainly it is, but it can be slowed by planting some bushes in a curved pattern along the path and by hanging a wind chime at your front door. You could also try placing two potted plants on either side of your front door. Be creative, but always be mindful of how the path feels. If it feels like the energy is rushing to your door, it probably is and should be addressed.

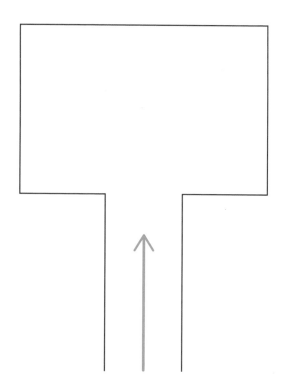

▲ The Challenge: This walkway is challenging because its straight, direct path creates an arrow that "attacks" the house with rushing chi.

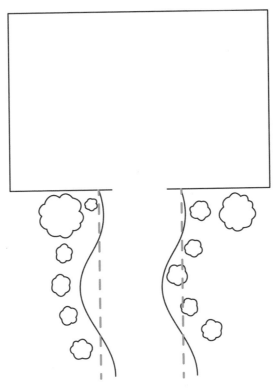

▲ The Cure: Correct the fundamental flaw by positioning a path of rocks in a curved, water-like pattern along the sides of the walkway, and by anchoring the door with a pair of potted plants.

If you use a side entrance to the house rather than the front door, you can treat it as your main entrance, especially when placing the bagua there as a starting point in feng shui. If you live in an apartment with a nonprivate entrance, you can still create a personalized pathway to your door by placing a small wind chime in front of your door or by positioning a small potted plant just outside of it.

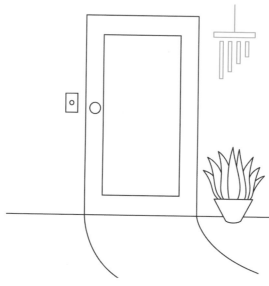

▲ The front door is the mouth of chi. Ideally, it should face the sun. If it doesn't, add wind chimes to represent positive flow.

ACCENTUATE THE POSITIVE

If you want to show the world that you are ready to receive any prosperity the universe might want to send your way, you can show it symbolically by adding the water element to your front yard. You could have a nice, big water fountain in the middle of a pond—or you could stay on the simple side and have a small bird-bath. Whatever you decide to use as your water element, be sure the water is directed toward your house rather than away from it, since water in feng shui equals wealth, and you don't want your wealth to be draining away from your house. You want to attract more wealth, of course!

There are a few other feng shui considerations in the front yard to be mindful of as you create a meaningful first impression to the world. For instance, the reason why a wind chime next to the front door is considered to be very auspicious is because it serves three purposes: First, it lets people know where you are. Second, it protects you by detecting when others are near. Third, it spreads good chi to all who come to your door.

As a final touch, consider placing a few potted yellow or red plants on either side of the front door, since that will extend the chi sideways a bit and spread it around your entire front door area.

Using the Bagua for Your Entryways

The bagua's energy map shows how energy flows through the physical world. To bring harmony and balance into your life, use this map to match the energy in your home to the different energetic patterns represented by the different sectors of the bagua. To do this, you'll first need to map the bagua onto your home, starting with your front doorway, so you know which areas of your home relate to which sectors.

Looking back at the bagua, you'll notice that in this school of feng shui you will always enter the home in one of three different sectors. Standing outside looking toward the door, it will be in either knowledge/wisdom to the left, career/life path in the center, or helpful people/travel to the right.

Picture your home as a big square or rectangle or even a tic-tac-toe board that divides your home into nine equal sections. Now align the bagua with your front door. If your front door is in the center of your home (like many center-hall colonials), then you'd be entering in the career sector of your home and the other sectors would follow suit accordingly. It's really this simple!

READING THE MAP

Now that you understand how to position the bagua, think about the deeper energies of each sector and how you can take the map from your front door through your life.

Career

The career corner can represent your career/job, but also your life path or your soul's purpose. Career can be represented by the water element, a meandering shape, or the color black.

If this area is lacking in your home's bagua, enhancements or cures to this sector would be anything relating to water, such as a fountain, an aquarium, a picture of water, or the color black. It doesn't need to be a lot—just remember it is your intention as you place the object that gets that energy moving for you.

Knowledge

Wisdom and spirituality are the fundamental keys to knowledge. The image of the mountain and the colors of blue, green, or black are representative of the knowledge corner.

Enhancements and cures begin with asking yourself what spirituality means to you, then adding that element to this sector. If you want to learn how to meditate, your knowledge center would be a wonderful area of your home or room to use. Surround yourself with things that help you to relax. Consider using a beautiful aromatherapy candle in the color blue (the most auspicious color for this sector), incense for your rosary recitation, a Buddha, or any other object that represents spirituality/self-knowledge to you. Creating this "sacred space" will be very helpful in tuning out the world and tuning in to your higher self.

Family

Your ancestry, or family heritage, is represented by the wood element, the colors green and blue, the image of thunder, and a vertical rectangular shape (like a column or tree trunk).

Enhancements or cures to use in the family sector include family photos, the element of wood, the color green (most auspicious), plants, trees, and heirlooms. Based upon your intention, you can use anything else that reminds you of your family in a positive way—even if it's to gently remind you to let go of the past.

Wealth

Cold, hard cash is nice, but wealth equals abundance in all things. In the bagua of your home, it's represented by the image of wind and the colors purple, red, green, and blue. Purple is the most auspicious color.

To enhance or cure any missing piece of this sector in your wealth corner, use anything that represents wealth to you. Think about what abundance really means to you and what form of it is lacking in your life. Many people associate wealth with having a lot of money, but true abundance takes many forms—and it's amazing how right when you begin to realize this, the green stuff begins to start flowing back into your life.

With respect to this area of the bagua, ask yourself the following questions: In which areas of your life do you feel abundant? Do you have control of your money or does it control you?

Fame

Fame, here, is not notoriety, but rather visibility or noteworthy presence. This recognition is represented by the element of fire, the shape of a triangle or pyramid, and the color red.

To determine your own fame, ask yourself: Do you feel you have something valuable to share with the world? How would others describe you? Do you feel visible? If your answers are negative in any way, you can enhance or cure the corresponding area by adding anything that represents fire and the color red. Simple items include red candles, pyramid-shaped objects, or representations of the sun. You can also incorporate awards or recognitions you have received for a job well done, or things that are self-esteem builders—perhaps something you've made that was a real challenge or accomplishment for you.

Relationships

The relationships corner represents love and commitment. Relationships, or their place in your life, are demonstrated by the image of earth and the colors pink, white, and red, with pink being the most auspicious.

If you are not experiencing perfect love, you can enhance or cure this corner by adding anything that reminds you of the love that does exist in your relationship or is representative of the love you are trying to create. Display a picture of you and your partner depicting happy times, or if you haven't found your partner, find a picture of a loving couple, symbolizing what you want in your life. If you are using objects, don't forget to pair items together—use two pink candles or two pink rose quartz stones, two lovebirds, or pictures of two people together. All are terrific items to use in your relationships corner as a means of attracting what you want.

Children/Creativity

This corner is represented by the metal element, or round or white items. The children or creativity sector can represent either children in your life or your inner child.

You can enhance or cure the area by thinking about what you really want to create. Maybe it's a new life for yourself, or a baby. Are you clear about your intentions, and have you given up any fears that may be holding you back? Sometimes clearing out a space for a new arrival can shift that energy. Or maybe you need something to remind you to relax—in which case, you might want to add a whimsical piece of art or a picture of yourself when you were a child having fun and being silly! Of course, you can also add anything in the metal element (maybe the picture frame) or the color white or something in a round shape.

Helpful People

The helpful people corner is also related to travel and is represented by the image of heaven and the colors gray, white, and black (with gray being the most auspicious). The sector is representative of friends, mentors, angels—basically anyone who has helped propel you on your life course!

To enhance or cure this corner, use pictures of friends, mentors, or teachers, or use things related to travel, such as art you've bought on a trip. Putting these kinds of items in this sector can help reflect more of that energy into this space. Heavenly objects work well here, so get out those angels and celestial symbols!

Health

Health is at the center of the home's bagua—and it's where all the energies of the other sectors combine and balance. Represented by the earth element, the health sector symbolizes your ability to nurture and support yourself. The shape is square, and the color associated with health is yellow.

If all is not really well and whole with your health, you can enhance or cure this area of your bagua by keeping this space as clear as possible. This is important, since it's a reflection of the state of your health. If you've been sick lately, you may want to place a picture of yourself in this area—of when you were feeling vibrant and alive—to remind your body, mind, and soul to try and return to that healthy state. Earthenware objects and the color yellow can also be used as good, healthy symbols in this sector.

The Energy of Entrances and Foyers

Much like the front door projects an image of you to the rest of the world, your entrance (foyer for some; lobby for those blessed with a larger entranceway) reflects the image of who you are *into* your house. It picks up on the energy of the front door and brings that image right on inside.

The entrance is still part of the mouth of chi; therefore, it's important to keep the airways open in the entranceway so that good chi can "breathe" throughout your home. If you have a large entrance to your home, you won't have to do much to enhance this area from a feng shui standpoint. But if your entrance is narrow, you would greatly benefit from a metal wind chime hung from the ceiling. The door, when opened, will immediately start circulating the chi, sending it out from your entrance to all areas of your home. If there's a window near your entrance, make sure you slow down the chi with some billowy curtains, miniblinds, or a plant in front of the window, especially if you've got a wind chime helping to spread good chi. You don't want it to go running out the window, right?

For hallways, the most common problem is that they are too narrow, which can be translated in feng shui to symbolize a narrow mind. Open up the space with hall mirrors and a round crystal to reflect light and double the space. The crystal will also help get the chi flowing in many directions.

Staircases are very important in feng shui, because they represent the arteries that carry energy throughout your home. If your door opens to a staircase that leads down a level, your positive chi will run down the steps; if it opens directly to a staircase (as is often the case in apartments), you'll get too much negative chi at once. Place a small mirror on the outside of your front door to shield yourself from the rush of negative chi.

If you have a staircase that appears challenging in any way, you can lessen the challenge by adding some visual elements like family pictures, décor items with a particular theme, or something that shows movement and progression. Using accents will provide the mental message of "You can do it!" to anyone who feels up to the task of climbing your stairs. You have a duty to create a pleasant journey for anyone brave enough to ascend!

Many feng shui practitioners agree that a good ratio for windows to doors is a three-to-one ratio. Too many windows can cause disruption and argument in a home and too few can be stifling. Skylights count as windows.

Chapter 4

The Living Room

The living room is a place where memories are made, but it's also where good memories are preserved. Call it "the museum of you." From family pictures on the mantel to that fabulous ottoman you reupholstered yourself, your living room symbolizes the harmony you have in every relationship in your life, from family to community.

Room for Living

In many homes, the living room is the first room everyone sees upon entering through the front door. Ideally, it is visible from many areas of your home, as it is considered the "hub" of energy in feng shui. The heart of your home—a place that holds your memories and spreads joy into the rest of your living space throughout the house—the living room should be clearly visible or easily accessible from other rooms. Keep in mind that wherever this room is located in your home's blueprint, it has an inherent family energy and should be decorated or enhanced accordingly.

The formal living room—the one reserved for special occasions and visits from friends, family, and "company"—has mostly become a thing of the past. And that's a good thing! Good feng shui means living life in flow with the universe, and life is way too short to spend hundreds of dollars decorating a living room that can't be lived in!

Your "room for living" should reflect who you are and who you would like to see yourself become. It's a place for dreaming and introspection and connection with the self as much as it is for connection with others.

Incorporate your family traditions into your living room too. Even if it means you watch football every Sunday in your living room or have a Friday night movie "date" with your significant other. The important thing is to create a warm, welcoming, and safe place for you and other members of your family to come together to share your hopes, dreams, and ideas in a receptive, caring environment. That's what your living room is really all about.

Preserving the Energy of This Space

———

Use wisdom and power to enhance this meaningful room. First, you need to look at the direction the room is in. The best energies for a living room in feng shui come from the south, southeast, or southwest. These directions inspire creativity, lively conversation, and the positive exchange of ideas. West is also a good location for entertaining, so focus on that area of the room when having a party or get-together in your living room.

Position furniture so that it supports one of the main purposes of the room: to build a strong sense of family cohesiveness and community. That means you should have your sofa and chairs positioned so that they face the center of the room. Allow family and guests to choose their own best direction to sit, but be sure that no one is placed with their back to an entrance or window; if need be, angle the piece so that your guest's back is protected by a corner or wall. You don't want your visitors to feel open and vulnerable. Remember that your guests all need to be able to see an entrance to the room from where they are sitting and you will be fine.

If you have lots of hard corners in your living room, try constructing tiny triangular-shaped shelves in the corners; then add decorative items in various shapes and textures. This will soften the edges of the room, lessening the effects of harshly converging chi.

With end tables, coffee tables, and the like, be sure to soften sharp angles or "poison arrows" by angling the softer pieces of furniture in a way that cushions or supports the sharper energy coming from such arrows. Watch for incomplete shapes in the form of furniture that is not well balanced. Use smaller pieces to complete square or rectangular shapes not accomplished by larger pieces grouped together.

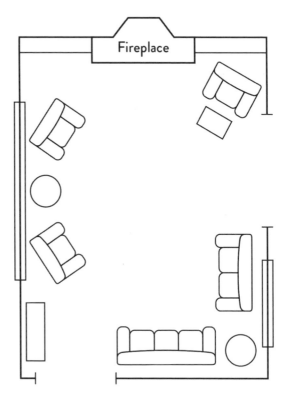

▲ Chi needs to move freely through the living room, but you should also position the furniture so that pieces are facing each other to facilitate conversation.

DECORATIVE ELEMENTS

The décor of the room should be warm colors, soft fabrics, and comfort-producing accessories such as plenty of soft pillows, blankets, or throws. Add an animal element such as a faux fur rug to add interest—or, better yet, let your real pets roam your living room. The chi will get really moving throughout the house as the animals move from one room to another!

Fireplaces add the fire element to the living room nicely, but keep in mind that the furniture should not face the fireplace if you want to promote harmonious relationships. Facing the fire can bring problems in the form of fiery confrontation.

Speaking of fire elements, make sure there is enough light in the hallways leading to your living room. Doing so is much like making sure the arteries to your heart are clear and open: It will help direct the healthy chi to the heart of your home.

Don't block a fireplace with a large, overstuffed sofa. Larger sofas work best in small rooms if they are placed sideways in a corner, with plenty of room to walk freely around them. Fireplaces should remain free and open, with very little around them.

Accent your living room with colorful artwork to boost the chi in the room, or you can use pastels to soften the room even more. The more colorful accent pieces work great for lively parties and entertaining, while the soft pastels enhance the room's more peaceful, meditative qualities. Choose whichever best suits your needs—the main idea is to have art and accessories that are pleasing for you and your guests to look at while you are engaged in meaningful conversation.

Ideally, the well-balanced living room will contain an invigorating mix of colors, shapes, and textures—a healthy dose of yin and yang opposites.

▲ Balancing Art: The mixture of circles (the round clock, mirror, and vase) and lines (the frames), as well as the mixture of metal, wood, and fire elements, brings a yin-yang balance to this mantel.

Engage people's interest by appealing to their senses as well. Add smell-enhancing aromatherapy items such as scented candles, oils, or potpourri; soft music or a water fountain to appeal to the sense of sound; and lighting in a variety of types to appeal to the sense of sight. Touch is covered by the soft fabrics in the room, and taste is represented by any food or beverage you choose to serve.

TAILOR THIS ROOM TO YOU

Imagine the sheer joy of waking up on a weekend with nothing to do except plop onto your sofa, kick up your feet, and read a good book, all the while sipping coffee, tea, or hot chocolate.

That's the feeling you want to experience in your living room day after day. You can start by keeping a journal of all the things you really like to do in your living room. That will tell you most clearly what kind of space you need to create in your "room for living."

For example, do you like to relax and read in your living room? If so, you'll need to create a small library of good books there, and place a soft, comfortable chair in the knowledge corner to increase the positive learning effects of your reading. Or maybe your living room is a place for rejuvenation of your health and spirit, in which case you might want to focus more on the health area or center of your living room. Here, you can place a small fountain and arrange your furniture in an octagonal shape to draw in all kinds of healthy, positive chi.

If you are uncertain about which changes to make, contact a qualified feng shui consultant. A great consultant can really get the chi moving—and can inspire your own creativity tenfold!

Think about what you are doing in your living room and why. Remember that good feng shui dictates that you practice mindfulness in every room of your house. Your living room, like any other room in your living space, needs to support your life goals while maintaining its other purpose, which is to create a strong sense of community. Working with this energy in mind, you can create a living room that both strengthens your personality and makes visitors feel as though they are welcome guests in your world.

THE "NO-WORK ZONE"

Above all else, be especially mindful of inadvertently mixing business with relaxation by letting your work find its way into your living room. It's amazing how quickly books, files, and even computers can grow legs and creep into your living room, disturbing the peace and disrupting your family life by adding an aura of chaos and mixed boundaries.

If you have been feeling a distance between yourself and your family members, work could be the culprit—check around the total living room area to be sure that there are no stray work papers, cell phones, or sticky notes to get between you and some quality family time.

CREATE INTENTIONAL BOUNDARIES

How do you really accomplish a "no-work zone" in your living room? By arranging your furniture in such a way that it promotes peace, harmony, relaxation, and communion with those closest to you.

Move the sofa and guest chairs in more of a square or octagonal position to create a strong sense of community and sharing— and to keep outside influences from entering that sacred space. It's much harder to bring your work into the living room when the furniture is arranged in this manner, and, from a feng shui standpoint, this is the position that solidifies healthy communication between family members. With solid communication in the family, there will be less of a need to sneak work into this space, and more of a need to stay balanced in your personal and professional lives.

Using the Bagua

In the living room, the bagua can be as alive as it would be in any other room or area of your home. Place the bagua at the main entrance to your living room with the career side aligned with the entrance wall. In which section of the bagua does the front doorway fall? More than likely, it will be in the following areas of the bagua: children, family, or knowledge. In any of these three areas, you'll want to include items that celebrate or relate to each of these main "bagua entrances."

You can also incorporate items that correspond to each area of the bagua in its specific corner or area of the room—this will strengthen or emphasize each, depending on your intention. If you want a stronger, more cohesive family life, you can focus more intently on the family corner of the bagua in your living room, for instance, by giving more attention to groupings of family photos on your mantel. If your mantel is not located in the family area, you can create a small space for a group of family photos on a table or shelf in that corner.

If you've had difficulties with a specific member of your family but want to make things better, try hanging a small crystal from the photo of that person, or burn a small stick of peacemaking lavender incense near that person's framed photo. Intentions are powerful, so expect things to happen just by focusing your attention in that direction!

In the bagua as it relates to your living room, you'll also want to pay particular attention to your wealth corner. Your living room is the life-giving heart of your home, so if you're concerned about the wealth of your family, this is a good room in which to activate some positive chi with respect to finances and abundance in general. To do this, hang a crystal or place a Zen fountain in the wealth corner of the living room.

If you don't have space for a fountain, or if it's not appealing to you to have such a water element in the living room, you can also hang a lucky bamboo flute, since wealth in feng shui is also symbolized by wind, and the flute is a wind instrument. A flute created in bamboo is doubly lucky, as according to Chinese tradition bamboo is one of the luckiest plants around.

In relation to the helpful people/travel corner of the bagua, you could focus your attention more on the travel aspect, since the dining room, which is often but not always adjacent to the living room, also symbolizes the helpful people in your life. You might include a photo of a favorite place your family has visited. For some, a picture of an archer shooting an arrow at a row of stars might symbolize goals and reaching for the stars (relating to this bagua corner's connection to the heavens). You will find what works best for you.

The children/creativity corner can have pictures of your children, gifts from your children, or even gifts from other children who are close or special to you. Remember that creativity is equally symbolic here. You don't need to have children to focus on the creativity this area can celebrate or bring to your life. In fact, many people who paint, quilt, or crochet hang their creations in this area of their living rooms as a way of sharing their talents with family, friends, and guests.

Using the bagua and your pure intentions, you can do wonders in the meaningful placement of furniture and accessories in your living room.

Let intention drive your choices. For instance, it may seem unusual to have a stereo in your relationships corner, but if music or dancing is important to you and your partner, then a music source is symbolically in keeping with your endeavors.

Incorporate the Elements

In addition to bringing the bagua to life in your living room, you should also focus on balance when revamping the room according to feng shui principles. Too much of one kind of element can greatly affect the balance in the room, which in turn can create blockages and stagnant chi. What you really want most of all is to balance the elements in a way that instantly creates a feeling of calm in the room. Remember, the living room is a space for peaceful relaxation as much as it is a space for warm gatherings with family and friends.

Here are some suggestions for boosting the chi with each of the five elements:

- **Fire.** To increase the representation of the fire element in your living room, use lots of the color red, light candles, or use your fireplace often. You can also boost the fire element in the room by adding spiky plants such as a cactus or ficus.

- **Wood.** You can add more of the wood element to your living room by incorporating more green as an accent color (maybe by including taller, treelike plants) or adding more wood, wicker, or bamboo in the form of furniture and accent pieces.

- **Earth.** Grounding your living room space with more earth elements can really enhance an ethereal space, such as a living room with a vaulted ceiling, skylights, and the like. To boost the earth energy in the room, you could add soft linen, cotton, or even silk pillows, draperies, or slipcovers, or add a throw in warm earth tones to your sofa. If you want even more earthiness, consider a clay pot or ceramic sculpture.

- **Metal.** Reflective metal lighting fixtures work well to increase the metal element within a living room, but you can also include items that are white or that are spherical. Think creatively as well as mindfully: Metal picture frames or sculptures can incorporate several elements.

- **Water.** The easiest way to boost the water element's energy in your living room is to add an aquarium. In feng shui, nine is an auspicious number, so it is highly recommended that you have nine fish in your aquarium at all times. If one dies, replace it immediately. If aquariums are not appealing to you, you can use a Zen water fountain, hang a mirror, or use black and blue colors to represent the water element in the living room.

Balancing the elements is very easy to do in each room in your home, beginning with the living room. Just remember that you have options. Take a literal approach and add each element by choosing an item that concretely depicts or symbolizes it. Or be more associative: Represent each of the five elements with the colors or shapes that correspond to them.

When you are creating balance in a room, you are creating harmony in your life—and that extends to the life of your family too.

Solving Common Living Room Problems

While living rooms can be the easiest rooms in your home in which to apply the principles of feng shui, they can also present some problems that can be turned into opportunities if handled the feng shui way. Here are some typical problems:

- **An unusually shaped room.** Maybe your living room isn't the perfect rectangular or square shape it ought to be in order to be in perfect balance with nature. But nature isn't perfect, either, so cure the issue of any "missing" corners of the room by hanging mirrors in the area they would be located in to create the illusion of corners. For living rooms with an extra corner, you can hide the additional area with large potted plants or pieces of furniture. If you choose furniture for such an area, be sure to curve it so that it faces the other pieces of furniture in the room; therefore, no one is ever left out of a conversation.

- **Bad mirror placement.** Sometimes, a mirror can be hung at a disadvantageous location in a living room (or anywhere else, for that matter). Don't place a mirror in a position where it will reflect the front door; this can send the good energies running, or absorb and reflect negative ones into the room. Use mirrors to enhance space, not simply to reflect it.

- **Bad views.** Does your living room have a window that over-looks an undesirable view? Maybe you live next door to a hospital or a waste dump. If you do, you can still practice good feng shui by blocking the negative view with a large plant.

- **Clutter everywhere.** Okay, the only cure for this is for you to roll up your sleeves and pitch the clutter. Get rid of things you no longer need, and put away the things that are useful to you but that block the energy of the room because they don't belong there. The living room is for living, not for burying yourself in the debris of your life!

- **Stuck sofas.** Position your sofa in a way that inspires free exchange of ideas and communication. Under a beam is a bad location, because it can cause headaches and make the person sitting on the sofa feel oppressed and vulnerable. Too close to a TV can also disturb relaxation periods, since the electricity can interfere with rest. Try to imagine your sofa as a soft oasis, an escape from the pressures of the world. Keep it from getting its positive energies stuck in bad positions.

- **Bad beams.** Beams create barriers and block energy everywhere, so they are not the best option in feng shui. You don't want to block your good fortune in life, so hide the overhead beams with a false ceiling or soft draperies. If you can, install a light or a ceiling fan on the main beam to keep chi flowing and to redirect the energy in the room.

- **Sunken living room.** Some people love sunken living rooms because they are a creative alternative to the norm—but in feng shui, sunken living rooms are something akin to the *Titanic*. Here, you are symbolically showing the world that you don't mind being stepped on, which means you will always be stuck in a subordinate job and never be paid what you're really worth. No hidden treasures here, but you can try to cure the space by placing a coffee table with a mirrored top in the center of the area—reflecting and elevating your energy back to a level of strength and power.

- **Secondary purposes.** If the space is used for a secondary purpose, other than as a center of community and family togetherness, be sure to find a way to section the secondary purpose off at times when the room is not used for that purpose. For instance, you might need to use the living room as an office at times, but you should either section your desk area off with a screen or some plants or buy a desk that has cupboards that totally enclose the workspace so that it is not visible when you are using the living room for its intended or primary purpose.

- **Noncentral living room.** What if your living room is not the hub of your home? Maybe you have an unusual layout in your home, one that places your living room in the basement or another noncentral area. If this is the case in your home, you can install a ceiling fan to dissipate the energy from your living room into other areas of your home, or you can use sound (stereo, fountain, or wind chime) to attract others to your living room location.

Pictures and photos reflect the things that are most important to you. Carefully choosing which pictures will hang in which areas of your home will have positive outcomes. For example, if you'd like to have better health, a picture of a lovely, healthy plant in your health corner will do wonders. Even better is a real healthy plant!

Creating a living room space that lives, breathes, and grows with the entire family is sometimes challenging work from a feng shui standpoint, but it is ultimately quite rewarding.

Chapter 5

The Dining Room

In accommodations that include one, the dining room is typically the most formal room of a home. It's where all the high-level entertaining and family discussion usually takes place—simply put, it's where a lot of the chi in your family gets moving!

Creating a Warm and Welcoming Atmosphere

In most traditionally designed homes, the dining room often falls in the helpful people corner of your bagua. This is no accident—often, it's the people who help you most in your life (family, friends, business associates) who are invited to your dining room for celebrations of all kinds. Whether you entertain with lavish parties several times a year or invite a few friends over for an intimate dinner once in a blue moon, you'll want your dining room to reflect the fact that you appreciate the helpful people in all areas of your life.

> Mirrors reflecting the dining room table are a way to symbolize abundance. If the food is magnified, it will symbolize plenty of healthy abundance for all who are seated around your dining room table.

Think about it for a moment: Many of your important life decisions and changes happen at a family discussion around the dining room table. People have filled out college applications, announced engagements and pregnancies, and talked about the future sitting at the table. For most families, many wonderful holidays and celebrations have taken place there as well. Memories are served with each and every dinner!

In feng shui, the dining room is a room full of symbolism that affects every important aspect of your life. Here, you can place items that remind you of or celebrate the people who have helped you in life, but you can also place photos or paintings of interesting places to travel—whether you have already been there or just hope to go—since the helpful people corner of the bagua also corresponds to travel.

Of course, if you have a dining room that is located in another area of the bagua, you can simply look at its corresponding life endeavor (such as career or self-knowledge) and incorporate symbolic items in the room. Remember that your intention is personal, so you can choose any items you'd like as long as they are symbolic for you.

Just because the helpful people corner is in the area of the bagua where most dining rooms fall does not mean you should focus only on those who can help you. You can also use it as a reminder of the many ways in which you can serve or help others.

So, how do you use feng shui to create a warm, spacious, and welcoming atmosphere? Start with the entrance to your dining room. Is it near the kitchen and the living room? It's good to have the dining room close to the kitchen, since going back and forth for food will not take you far from your guests' enchanting company. The closer your dining room is to the living room, the more comfortable your guests will feel mingling with others—especially if you've grouped people from different areas of your life, mixing family, friends, and coworkers. Like healthy chi, your guests will want to flow in and out of rooms rather than be kept prisoner in one small room of your home!

Be mindful of maintaining a properly flowing chi. It is best if you have at least one window in your dining room to help fresh chi come in, but if you have two windows, you might want to use draperies, miniblinds, or even beaded curtains to slow down rushing chi. Otherwise, your guests might come and go like the wind!

If your dining room doesn't have windows, a chandelier or a small ceiling fan will help circulate the chi in your dining room. Best if your chandelier has a round crystal ball hanging from it!

In terms of décor and furnishings, remember that the dining room is like a fine restaurant within your home. You'll want it to appear fancy and worth the visit, but also very clean. Assuming you have no clutter in your dining room, consider the following elements of décor and ways you can enhance the ambience with mindful use of feng shui.

LIGHTS
When it comes to lighting, less is most often more. You might want to install a dimmer switch so you can have more light in the daytime and soft, romantic light in the evening. Of course, candles add the fire element to your evenings of entertaining, and they provide a calming, warm, and inviting energy. Don't forget to share the warmth. Take the opportunity to have "romantic" candlelit dinners in the dining room with your children or your friends. Remember that any night you spend with people who are important to you is a night worth celebrating!

DRAPERIES
Windows are critical elements in controlling flowing chi. For window treatments, you definitely want soft and flowing. Your draperies shouldn't cover the window completely, but serve to slow

down the chi and soften the windows. If you are concerned about too much sunlight or not enough privacy, install fabric shades or miniblinds so that you can let the chi back in when you want it.

If there are too many windows in your dining room,
hang a drapery or pull a shade while entertaining.
Too many windows can be very distracting for guests,
who will become more focused on passersby
than on your meaningful conversation!

FLOORS

Wood floors are ideal in a dining room, because they really ground the energy in the room, and depending on the levels of energy you have, this may be an absolute necessity! Enhance your wood with a colorful area rug, since color improves appetite and is considered good for digestion.

Try to avoid wall-to-wall carpeting, because it absorbs a lot of energy and can bog down the room. Not only will the carpeting give the room a heavy feeling, but it will make your guests feel full well before their stomachs are at capacity. If you do have wall-to-wall carpet in your dining room, try placing a multicolored area rug under the table to add interest and dilute the heaviness.

ART AND ACCESSORIES

Choose interesting and conversation-worthy art and accessories with which to adorn your dining room. A large print of a watercolor that features a young woman getting her palms read by a fortune-teller will add a little folklore to your helpful people corner, while a painting or item that represents your favorite destination is mindful of the travel aspect. You can include paintings that speak to you—and that you don't mind talking about—in your dining room.

Create a calm, relaxing atmosphere for yourself and your guests. If you have an overstimulating dining room, it can disrupt the digestion of everyone at the table. Moderation in all things, including décor!

Handmade work by local artisans can really add an earthier feel to the room. Incorporate some functional art you've collected, such as handmade serving dishes, handblown wineglasses, or one-of-a-kind silverware. This is your shining opportunity to share such loveliness with others, so pull it all out for a lively evening of entertaining!

Be Mindful of the Energy Flow

When the energy flow of your dining room is favorable, the flow of conversation improves, too, and you, your family, and your guests will have an appetizing and stimulating meal without even realizing how much the arrangement and décor of your dining room is contributing to your sense of satisfaction. But a dining room that does not have good chi is one in which guests eat quickly and depart early and neither the taste of the food nor the table talk lingers.

For your dining room, consider a round table. Round tables make people feel more at ease, encourage conversation, and ensure that no one has to take the "head" position, which can feel intimidating in someone else's home. Also, rounded, smooth lines and curves encourage smoother energy flow. Also remember to leave enough room for guests to easily get into and out of their chairs, as well as to turn to speak to other guests. The table should be made of wood or metal, which offer good support, rather than more distant, less inviting marble or glass.

When arranging furniture in the dining room,
be sure that chairs don't restrict anyone from moving easily
through doorways. There should be ample space for
guests to walk to and around the table.

Avoid having clocks in your dining room if you don't want your family and guests to feel rushed. Lighter colors are easier on your digestion, but some red can help inspire conversation. Abstract art is better placed in another room, unless you want your guests distracted by puzzling over what it represents. Still lifes of food or happy family gatherings—especially family photos of good times—are much more appropriate.

Applying the rules of feng shui, you can make your dining room a feast for the eye and a warm and relaxing place to nourish and entertain those you care about most.

PLACING YOUR GUESTS

When having a dinner party or holiday celebration, good feng shui dictates that your most important guest should sit facing the main entrance to the room—never with his or her back to the entrance, as this is the vulnerable position. You never want your most honored guest to feel vulnerable in your presence! Use the energy of direction to determine who should sit in which position—and then use placeholders with name cards so that each person knows they were intentionally seated at your table.

If you have a quiet, shy, or introverted person, position him or her in a southeast chair that faces northwest. The yang energy of this direction will encourage your guest to open up and join in the conversation.

East facing west is the traditional Chinese position of the eldest son, so it has an aura of ambition and power attached to it. It's also the romance position, with a little power and drama combined. It is an auspicious chair to find oneself in.

Younger children fare better in chairs that are located in the northeast corner of the table, and benefit from facing the encouraging energy of the southwest. This location is best for those who need a little encouragement or motivation in life.

Those who sit in the northern chair while facing south balance yin stillness with yang passion and excitement, making it a wonderful place for an attractive older person to sit.

Leaders should sit in chairs that are positioned northwest but that face southeast. In ancient (and often modern) China, this is where the "yang" father of the home traditionally sits—a strong position of power and leadership!

The "yin" mother in Chinese homes traditionally sits in the southwest corner of the table, facing northeast. This gentle energy is smooth going for family chi.

The traditional position of the ingénue, or attractive young woman, fares best when seated opposite the traditional eldest son position, or sitting west but facing east. Here, attraction is tempered by the playful, almost teasing, energy of the east. This is a great place to seat anyone who is looking to meet someone new—at your dining room table, of course.

Your most intriguing guest should probably sit south facing north, since this is the position of mystery and quiet ways.

Traditionally associated with the middle daughter in Chinese families, this chair's position will bring out the most expressive and interesting conversation in the whole room. Save this chair for a person who is lively, fun, and interesting—and who will likely lead the conversation along as smoothly as a babbling brook over rocks.

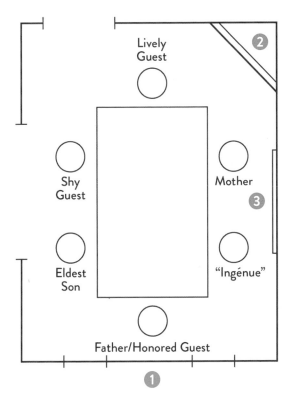

▲ ❶ The father/honored guest is seated in the least vulnerable position. ❷ A corner cupboard softens the hard lines of the room and the rectangular table. ❸ A mirror opposite the open arch makes the room seem more spacious, and also reflects back to those with their backs to the arch.

Keep in mind that, many times, people don't need to be strategically placed at your table. As an experiment, have a dinner party where there are no placeholders and everyone chooses his or her own chair. Note where each type of personality chooses to sit—it probably won't be too far off from the suggestions included in this chapter!

An even number of chairs around the table is best in feng shui, since it represents balanced energies and inclusiveness.

Remember Your Intention

Now that you know who should sit where, it's time to take a look at what kind of energy you want overall at your party—yin or yang? A yin party is ideal for quiet get-togethers, informal lunches, or everyday family meals where you want the rest of the world to stay away for a little while. Yang parties are best for formal occasions where you want lots of creative energies to blend. Follow these tips:

THE YIN DINNER PARTY

Low-key lunches, dinners, or family get-togethers are yin parties. For these, you'll want to decorate your table using yin elements:

- Wooden utensils (and chopsticks, if serving dishes that warrant their use).
- Wicker, bamboo, or cork place mats to ground the energy even more.

- Napkins, a tablecloth, and linens in pinks, blues, or greens (natural fibers work best).

- Wood chairs covered in soft cushions in pale colors.

- Wooden or earthen tableware (dishes, serving plates, and so on).

- A live plant as a centerpiece, symbolizing good health.

- Foods that contain water (salads and fruits).

To further enhance a quiet yin get-together, use soft music such as bamboo flute, soft piano, or even nature sounds. Keep the lights dimmed, and turn off electrical disturbances such as a TV or static-filled radio. Keep sharp objects stored neatly away when not in use.

THE YANG DINNER PARTY

Yang parties are those fantastic soirees that we all look forward to having once in a while. Lively, well-traveled guests provide intellectually stimulating conversation at yang parties. You will usually serve wine and cheese, and you have plenty of exciting artwork around to keep everyone's interest and energy high. However, a sparsely furnished room enhances all this excitement—leaving the evening wide open to great possibilities.

For your invigorating yang party, you'll want to decorate your table using yang elements:

- Square place mats (especially if your table is round).

- Reflective surfaces such as sparkling crystal and sterling silverware (of course, a mirror under your food will make it appear twice as plentiful too).

- Napkins, a tablecloth, and linens in bright colors (splashes of red to bring in the yang fire element).

- Sturdy metal chairs with brightly colored seat cushions (red or orange will surely light a fire under your guests to keep things lively and energetic).

- Fine china to exude an aura of wealth and prosperity.

- A centerpiece with roses and candles to ignite passion and romance.

- Yang foods such as spicy Cajun dinners, whole grain breads, smoked salmon, or peppered steak (a nice, hearty red wine such as a Cabernet Sauvignon or even Burgundy can finish out the yang energy in your food offerings).

Yang dinner parties require exciting and creatively inspiring music such as modern jazz, classical music, or even some rock and roll. With a yang party, the idea is to live it up as much as possible!

Typical Dining Room Problems

In feng shui, every problem area is a place full of opportunity. You simply need to identify the problem, then cure it with a feng shui solution that reverses the negative energy the problem caused.

THE FURNITURE

One of the most typical problems in the dining room is a table with sharp, pointed edges. Here, the solution is simple: Use soft linens to cover the table, or position the table diagonally in the room to lessen the effect of the poison arrows.

Another problem that often occurs is furniture that is not a comfortable fit—for your guests or the table. If your chairs don't fit smoothly under the table in your dining room, it may be time to purchase some new ones. And while rustic antique chairs may seem to add ambience, they can detract from the positive flow of chi in the room if they are not in good shape.

Table size can be a problem for those who like to eat at the dining room table, even when there isn't anyone else to join in the meal. For times when you are dining alone, you can cure the problem of seating imbalance by creating the illusion that others are dining with you. Drape the table linens over half the table, and group some photos together at the opposite end of the table. Add a living plant as an additional "guest" at the table.

When entertaining, don't use tall centerpieces, wobbly tables or chairs, powerfully fragrant candles (they'll interfere with the smell of wonderful cooking), or irritating music. Beams over tables are considered very inauspicious and should also be avoided in the dining room.

Tabletops should be smooth and easy to clean. If you have an old wooden tabletop with lots of grooves in it, food particles can get stuck in your table for an eternity—creating lots of stuck energy. If it's not easy to clean, cover the table with something that is.

THE ROOM

If you live in a smaller home or apartment, your dining room may not be as easily identifiable as it might be in a larger home with a separate dining room. In such smaller spaces, you can create a dining room with its own energy by separating the table area off with a screen, area rug, or even a group of indoor plants. This way, you'll create a dining space that has energies all its own. Or make the table itself the dividing line.

You can also create a separate space for special-occasion dining outside by joining some trellises and draping them with soft, pastel fabric coverings. This is an especially good thing to try for a romantic outdoor dinner for two. Just be sure to use a small, cozy table for two, and bring your dinner items out on a small cart or tray. Add a string of lights to bring illumination to the conversation!

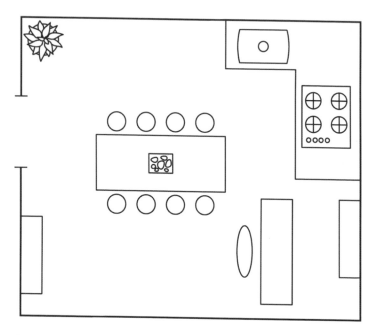

▲ In a smaller space without specific boundaries between kitchen, living, and dining areas, try positioning the dining room table set as the dividing line by placing it horizontally between kitchen and living room areas.

Always use soft lighting in your dining room, as well as soft colors such as greens and yellows. This softness will help keep the energy in the dining room flowing and positive, especially if you have guests who are prone to incite arguments.

MIRRORS

The issue of mirrors can be equally good or bad for a dining room. While mirrors are good for enhancing the feeling of wealth and abundance in the dining room, stay away from mirrors that are large and heavy. You don't want to overpower people with an exaggerated image of your abundance.

Mirrors can be especially disruptive to dinner parties if they reflect activity outside of the room—or worse, outside of the house. You don't want your guests looking at everything but the meal in front of them. Before you know it, they'll be looking at their watches too.

For meals, you should alternate the use of the kitchen and the dining room. This will activate the chi in both rooms, filling them with the loving rays of your family's energy and greatly increasing your family's prosperity in the meantime!

CLUTTER

Clutter in the dining area is bad feng shui, because it blocks your potential for wealth and prosperity. The dining room and the kitchen are both symbolic of the wealth in your family, and clutter is stagnant chi comprised of unfinished business and decisions that have yet to be made. With that much inertia, how could you ever go places in the world? Don't let your dining room table become a dumping ground for all your past and current projects. It is a place of honor in your home, and if you don't honor the space, how can you expect to receive any beneficial energy from it?

Chapter 6

The Kitchen

Good feng shui in the kitchen depends on many things, but most of the importance rests on harmony, balance, and mindfulness—both in design and practice. After all, the kitchen is the informal, yet critical, center of your home, where everyone gathers to eat, talk, and plan for the future. It's where meals and dreams are often shared. The kitchen is the core source of your family's wealth, health, and prosperity, so it should be treated with the utmost reverence.

Clear Your Kitchen

First and foremost—as in all areas of feng shui—you don't just start designing or redesigning your kitchen without clearing the unnecessary clutter first. Clean out your cupboards, donate food you don't want to homeless shelters, and pitch the things you don't need anymore. You'll be surprised how much lighter this will make you feel, and how much it will help your prosperity when you give up the need to hoard.

Keep your kitchen clean, because it represents prosperity in the form of good health and wealth. Dirty dishes, stoves, and refrigerators can block your abundance in these important aspects of your life, and they can also cause digestive problems in your body. Dirt can "clog" the arteries of your soul, making you feel unhealthy physically *and* financially.

Food should be stored away when not being used for cooking. You should use metal or wood canisters to store bread, flour, and sugar, especially if your storage canisters will be located between the stove and the refrigerator. This will balance your elements of fire (stove) and water (fridge) with a little wood and metal in between.

> To cultivate good chi, you must harmonize the five elements in your kitchen: wood, fire, earth, metal, and water.

Speaking of refrigerators, you can also apply the principles of good feng shui to the inside of your cold food storage. Use the bagua to determine which foods best correspond with each element—or simply go by the usefulness factor. If you sort food by its symbolism and usefulness to you and your family, you will always keep the things you need within close reach, and you will begin to practice the kind of mindfulness that helps you instinctively remove the things you don't need or use.

Practicing mindfulness will make a huge difference in lightening your mind and your body. You will store only the foods you know you'll use, effectively eliminating the kind of refrigerator clutter that makes people pack on extra pounds out of boredom.

Implementing Design

Once you are starting with a clean kitchen slate, you are ready to design a functional kitchen that allows plenty of good chi to flow through it. A "feng-tional" kitchen will invigorate and nourish all the inhabitants of your home. It will allow the maximum amount of good chi, neither stagnant nor rushing, to pass through it.

Chi that moves too quickly through the house can represent quickly draining finances. Rushing chi needs to be slowed down using a variety of cures such as butler doors, potted plants, or screens. Barriers like doors, which can open and close, are good chi slowers, as are mobiles and plant carts.

Stagnant chi is much more problematic in the kitchen and bathrooms than in any other areas of your house, because it can symbolically affect your health and finances. Stuck energy can manifest in your bank account as an inability to increase wealth, and in your stomach as difficulty digesting food properly. Get chi moving in these rooms by adding a small ceiling fan, hanging a crystal, or placing a small fountain in a corner of the room.

A kitchen that faces your front door is thought to be in a less-auspicious location, unless you are in the food preparation or catering business. It's a little too head-on to the chi, and you don't want the chi to hit you square in the forehead as you cook! The ideal direction for the cooking area of your kitchen to face is north.

The stove or oven (yang fire elements) should be located at least 2 feet away from the refrigerator or kitchen sink (yin water elements). When you have two opposite elements in close proximity, they will cancel each other's energy out. The oven should not face the kitchen door, either, since this will let too much "heat" out into your home.

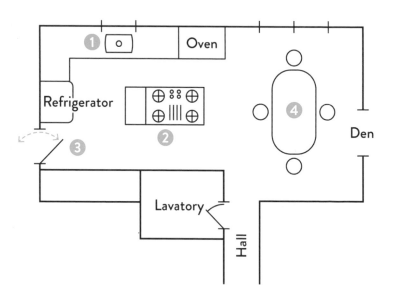

▲ ❶ The stove and sink are not too close. ❷ The person cooking can see all the doorways from one position. ❸ A swinging door to the dining room prevents the chi from rushing straight through the kitchen. ❹ The table set off to one side slows guests down and creates a more intimate setting for family meals.

A stove should face inward and contain reflective metal elements if this positioning puts you with your back to a door. If the stove has you with your back to a side door or back door, consider items like metal canisters or a metal utensil holder so you are not vulnerable and can see anyone approaching from behind you. A small mirror would work well here too.

Alternate use of the burners on your stove to keep your prosperity well balanced. Many cooks favor the two burners toward the front of the stove simply because they are closer, but it is best in feng shui to spread the energy around to maintain balance.

A final note about your stove: It should not face a bathroom or bedroom door. A stove too close to a bedroom wall can pose a fire threat to you and your family. The ideal location for a stove is in the open and not positioned under low ceilings or tucked into tight corners.

The stove is symbolic of wealth and prosperity in feng shui. You cannot grow and prosper without a way to cook your food. The more burners the better, and placing a mirror or reflective object that doubles their appearance helps too.

ADDITIONAL CONSIDERATIONS

For aesthetic reasons more than feng shui, your cooktop should not be placed in front of a window (particularly if it has a screen) since this reduces the airiness and openness of the design. Also, the front of your cooktop shouldn't face an entrance to your kitchen, since this would make it difficult for you to effectively greet all who enter your kitchen in hopes of fellowship and a good meal.

Another area worthy of attention in your kitchen is that of furniture. Do you have too much stuff in too small a space? Such a situation can block your chi. Open the room up by moving out pieces you don't absolutely need!

Overall, your kitchen should be light, open, airy, and as spacious as possible. It will make your guests feel welcome while increasing your own sense of health and well-being.

OPEN THE AIR

Ventilation is another area worth consideration in the "feng-tional" kitchen. Cooking delectable dishes may bring the unpleasant "aftertaste" of thick, smoke-filled air that lingers long after the meal has been digested. Install a ceiling fan if you don't have over-the-stove ventilation; an overhead fan will keep the air (and chi) circulating throughout the kitchen and its surrounding areas.

If you live in a place where you cannot install a ceiling fan, consider opening windows and hanging a wind chime in the window over your sink. This will also work well as a cure for stagnant cooking-related air.

For both feng shui and safety reasons, you should be sure to check your kitchen for proper airflow on a regular basis. Removing grease and food debris from your cooktop regularly can also help cut down on the smoke-filled air that can pollute your kitchen, block good chi, and choke your prospects for wealth.

OPTIMIZE LIGHT AND COLOR

Light and color are very important to the development of a healthy and "feng-tional" kitchen. If you have few windows in your kitchen, light is even more important to generate lots of positive chi. You should always have plenty of overhead lighting in your cooking and eating areas, and it is best to use full-spectrum lighting that is closest to outdoor lighting. Never use fluorescent lighting in your kitchen, since it is oppressive. Ceiling fans with lights in them work well, because they allow you to alternate light and motion, or use them full-strength together.

In terms of color, earth colors work best in kitchens. Green is associated with life and growth, so it is an ideal kitchen color. Country blues, beiges, and warm tones are okay as a second choice, provided there's lots of good lighting. Stark, white kitchens should be avoided—not only do they look clinical in Western culture, but in Asian culture, white represents death and mourning. If your kitchen is mostly white, you can balance it well with brightly colored pictures of healthy fruits and vegetables. This will bring vibrant energy to your kitchen!

In Asian culture, white represents death and mourning. If your kitchen is mostly white, bring in other elements, brighter colors, and items that symbolize health and life.

Enhancing Your Kitchen's Chi

The kitchen is the hearth and the stomach of your home, and it's especially important for that room to have good chi. Try the following:

- Eliminate clutter. Throw away what you can't use; donate or recycle what will serve others.

- Keep your kitchen clean, since it represents prosperity in the form of good health and wealth.

- Maintain ventilation to circulate chi and clear the room.

- Allow the maximum amount of good chi to pass freely through your kitchen, invigorating and nourishing all of the inhabitants of your home.

- Light and color are very important. Overhead, full-spectrum lighting is best.

- Earth colors (like forest green, which is associated with growth), balanced with bright white, work best in kitchens.

- Cook up good chi using the freshest ingredients. Buy only what you know you will use. Balance meat with fresh vegetables, and appeal to all senses throughout each dining experience.

- Include ancestors in the family dining experience, through photos, recipes, or a place at the table, and give thanks to the universe for every meal so that you will continue to be blessed.

As you continue to use feng shui, certain practices will become habit. Occasionally review the list, however, to remind yourself of your intentions, and refocus your energies where needed.

The Elements in Your Kitchen

To cultivate good chi, you must harmonize the five elements in your kitchen: wood, fire, earth, metal, and water. Since water represents prosperity and wealth, be sure that your kitchen faucets are not leaky. Leaky faucets are sure to "drain" your finances!

In addition to the sink, your refrigerator represents water in your kitchen, so make sure it's in good running order as well. The "fire" element of the stove is balanced by the "water" of your refrigerator and sink, so you're covered there. Remember to balance the other three elements too.

A HEALTHY KITCHEN

Wood is the most powerful element in cultivating good health from your kitchen. In your décor, you can use wood elements such as paneling, plants, wooden paper towel holders and other wooden kitchen accessories, and any décor item that serves up an image of wood elements (including trees or paper, and blue or green tones).

Your prosperity can also benefit from the addition of wood elements like bowls of fruit, pots of fresh herbs or vegetables, a collection of wooden utensils, or vases with flowers. (You may prefer silk flowers, since fresh flowers can represent death due to their rapid deterioration.) The options here are multiple; you'll want more than one of each wood element to attract prosperity, since like attracts like in the abundance game.

Do not overuse symbols of prosperity in the hopes of attracting more money. An overzealous nature can create negative chi and counteract your intention. Be strategic and purposeful in your placement.

REFLECTIVE ALTERNATIVES

Metal objects, because of their reflective properties, are useful for enhancing smaller nooks and hidden corners of your kitchen. Metal canisters work well in a small pantry or breakfast nook. However, metal knives should never be stored out in the open, whether hung on walls or in any kind of glass enclosure. When knives are left out in plain view like this, practitioners say that there will be many arguments and much pain in the household. Store your knives and other sharp objects in clay earthenware, in a wooden knife block, or in a drawer safely tucked away.

Proper use and balance of the five elements of feng shui is critical to the success of each room, but especially in the kitchen. Take a look around your kitchen to see how many elements you've already balanced instinctively—you'll be surprised by how much feng shui there is just because something seemed to feel right.

Be sure to open your heart and trust the process. Be clear about your intentions; trust your instincts to know what is right for you. When you walk into a room and do not feel comfortable in that space, most likely it is because the chi is stagnant or rushing through, which means it will require a cure.

Don't let the fact that you have a small kitchen limit you. Consider using a mixture of elements to open your space and keep the feng shui moving. When you use metal objects (for their reflective energies) and balance them out with wood, you'll end up with a nice chi going in your tiny space.

In the right environment, you may be inspired to cook more often—something you probably didn't do before. Good use of feng shui principles in your kitchen should inspire you to "nest" and even try new things. The positive, creative yang energy will be grounded and balanced when it is complemented by fresh yin cabinetry.

CREATE A SENSORY EXPERIENCE

What makes for a total feng shui kitchen experience? Nice use of all elements, coupled with a balance of items that appeals to all of the senses. Taste is enhanced, of course, by the wonderful foods you cook; smell can be positively affected by the same or by adding a simmering potpourri. Use soft chair covers or a silky tablecloth to appeal to touch. Good use of color and light in your kitchen, as well as in your food, is visually appealing.

For the all-important sense of sound, play some classical or jazz music for your dining pleasure, or you can run a smooth Zen fountain in the background. Although if you already have a fountain somewhere else in your house (such as in the wealth corner of your living room), you may be able to hear it clearly in the kitchen while you are eating.

Remember, also, that a clean, clutter-free kitchen positively impacts the sense of sight.

Remember Your Roots

One final area of kitchen feng shui that is often lost in modern translation is the reverence and inclusion of ancestors in the family dining experience. In ancient China, such reverence was prominent. Families often had altars dedicated to their ancestors in their homes, and thanked their ancestors for their contribution to the family's wealth and happiness.

In modern times, people may not have an ancestral altar in or near their kitchens, but they can still find nice ways of including ancestral energy in family mealtimes by doing simple things:

- Group old family photos and hang or place them in the helpful people corner of your kitchen, using the bagua with the front center positioned at the entrance of your kitchen to find the correct location.

- Place a recipe box filled with old family cooking secrets in your family corner, again using the bagua.

- Use kitchen implements that have been handed down. Inherited cooking utensils and kitchenware will bring you great comfort as you cook for your friends and family.

Certain ancestors or family members warrant special consideration. If you've recently lost an important relative, you might consider keeping a place at the table open for that person's spirit. You needn't use a place setting, but rather you could include a small potted plant at that end of the table to signify life that goes on. A hopeful act to honor the transition of a loved one can be a very healing experience.

Common Kitchen Problems

A common feng shui problem in the kitchen is if the kitchen door faces a bedroom door and the bedroom door (and stove) can be seen from the foot of your bed. Not a good idea, since in traditional Chinese culture, this particular position represents the "taking of the dead." In other words, if you died in your sleep, you'd likely be carried out this way! Move your bed so that it is at an angle, away from the stove and doors.

Meandering energy can create distraction for the cook—distraction that can cause disharmony and even safety problems in the kitchen. Rushing chi in a kitchen can make its inhabitants restless and unfocused, leading to kitchen injuries and mishaps.

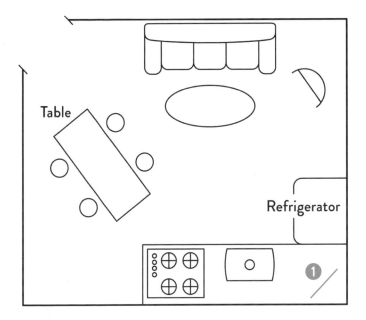

Table

Refrigerator

▲ If your stove puts you with your back to an entrance, hang a mirror above it (❶) so that you are not in a vulnerable position. You may also want to position the mirror so that it reflects the burners on your stove—that is said to increase your wealth by magnification!

Finally, consider the traffic pattern in your kitchen. If you have a kitchen island in the center of your kitchen, this can be the best design because it is the most open. The only time this is not true is where there isn't sufficient seating near the island. For example, what will happen if, in the center of a large, open kitchen, there is a kitchen island that faces two wide-open walls going into two other rooms? This kitchen, the nourishing center of a home, does not invite people to stay still for very long; instead, it encourages pacing and constant motion. The broader effects of that can be reflected in guests and family members who similarly wander into and out of your life.

Make Your Kitchen the Best It Can Be

To make sure your kitchen is the best it can be from a feng shui standpoint, here are the minimal essentials:

- Wood floors and lots of wooden cooking utensils or storage bins. Wood energy is fantastic in the kitchen, especially for floors. Ceramic tile is very yang and can make you feel tired and overwhelmed in your kitchen.

- Proper placement of critical appliances. Be mindful of where you place any new addition, even if it's just a coffee maker. Every new piece affects the energy in your kitchen differently and must be balanced properly to maximize its positive effects.

- Good housekeeping. Keep your kitchen and all of its surrounding areas clean and clutter-free.

- Regular disposal of useless items. Always toss broken or chipped dishes and plates. Imperfections like these attract stagnant or negative chi. According to Chinese folklore, keeping anything broken or useless in the kitchen shows a lack of respect for yourself and your food, and leaves you vulnerable to illness.

- Good balance of elements and energy: open, airy opportunities for good chi, combined with a good use of the five elements. Use a mutable element between two opposites; for instance, place a pot of fresh herbs (earth) between a stove (fire) and refrigerator (water) that are too close to one another.

- Fresh fruit and flowers. Keeping bowls of fresh fruit and flowers can attract positive chi into your kitchen and food. Just be sure to throw out anything that starts to deteriorate.

- Mindfulness and purpose. Always take inventory of what you use and how you use it in your kitchen. This same mindfulness applies to the kitchen itself: How do you really use this room, and how can you best arrange things to enhance and support that use?

Above all else, your "feng-tional" kitchen should be a place you enjoy spending time in, a place where you and your family can feel healthy, alive, and whole. Spending a lot of time evaluating your kitchen and using feng shui principles to enhance its potential can be a joyful and enlightening experience for the whole family!

Chapter 7

The Bathroom

If the front door of the home is the mouth of chi and the kitchen is the stomach, the bathroom is without doubt the internal plumbing or intestines of chi. This plumbing ties in to your personal chi as well, and you can suffer from an ill-positioned bathroom unless you pay attention to the finer details.

More than anything else, the bathroom is used for cleansing. Either you are cleansing the outside of your body in a bath or shower, or you are cleansing the inside of your body by expelling waste. So, it follows that your bathroom itself should be as clean as possible. Your bathroom, simply put, is a metaphor for how you care about yourself in terms of cleanliness, which is even more about how you present yourself to the outside world.

The Forgotten Room

The reality is that whether the bathroom is large or small, opulent or humble, few people take the time to decorate it, never mind use feng shui. The idea is not to spend too much time there, especially if you have more than one child and only one bathroom! Spending money to decorate the bathroom is almost always an afterthought, something to do only after you've spent lots of time, energy, and money sprucing up every other room in your home.

But there is that one cold splash-in-the-face of reality in feng shui: Your bathroom can be a major source of money loss if you don't pay attention to it. It can also affect your health in ways you would prefer not to think about, especially if your bathroom is located in the center of your home's bagua, which is the health area. Traditional Chinese homes were built with enclosed courtyards in the center of them, and this was a place of spiritual contemplation and meditation. So the ancient Chinese would have found it terribly distasteful to perform other bodily functions in this sacred space.

Although the ancient Chinese didn't have modern facilities in their homes, the basic philosophies of feng shui that pertain to sacred space—as well as water and its significance—still apply. You should, at the very least, practice mindfulness in the design and décor of your bathroom, or you will run into problems with health and financial well-being.

LOCATION, LOCATION, LOCATION

The best direction for your bathroom to face is north, because that direction's corresponding element in feng shui is water, and water is a good thing in the bathroom since it is for washing and cleansing. If your bathroom faces a different direction, such as south (which represents fame, reputation, and recognition— qualities you'd rather not be flushing away), you can place a mirror on the wall opposite the north side of the room to reflect northern energy into the room.

Mirrors are always good for opening up small, cramped bathrooms into seemingly larger and more appealing ones. Just be mindful of where you place them, so not only light but also good chi are reflected in the right direction.

The ideal location for a bathroom is away from the wealth and health sectors of the home bagua. If it's in the wealth corner, you'll need to use more cures to keep your finances from going down the drain. The health corner is in the center of the home, and fortunately, not many homes are designed with bathrooms in this particular location. Still, if yours is one that happens to defy the odds, you can hang a crystal in the doorway of the bathroom to activate healthy chi all around you while you are indisposed. This will especially help if you have digestive or intestinal problems.

Other less-auspicious locations for bathrooms include bathrooms facing kitchens, bedrooms, or meditation rooms/altars; and bathrooms located on the second floor just above the main entrance door downstairs. If your bathroom is in any of these positions, read the list of possible cures you can use to open the chi and correct the space. For more cures, see the section on "Adding the Eight Remedies or Cures" in Chapter 1.

Also give consideration to the position of the bathtub or shower. Just as with other areas in your home, you never want your back facing a doorway—it's a position of vulnerability, and someone could sneak up on you. The same is true if your doorway opens to face the tub or shower head-on. If your bathtub or shower puts you in either of these less-than-ideal situations, try positioning a small mirror inside the shower area (the wall-mounted variety that can be extended work great for this). You could also try to section the area off with a screen or with soft draperies to give you a little more privacy.

If your bathroom location puts you in a vulnerable position, hang a small bamboo chime near the door. The sound and movement of the chime will keep the chi flowing and will also alert you to nearby motion. The bamboo represents wood, which balances water's energy.

Use Mindful Décor in the Bathroom

Before you can begin to address the things in your bathroom, it is important to first clear and clean it. Begin by clearing the countertop of any item you don't need, even if it looks good there. In feng shui, you ultimately want things that are visually appealing yet useful to you in some way, even if their only purpose is to balance elements or slow down rushing chi. Color is also important to the cleanliness issue, because too much color in the bathroom can make it appear full and unsanitary.

LIGHTING
Be mindful of lighting when creating a healthy bathroom. Too much bright light can be disturbing and offensive; too little can be depressing. Ideally, your bathroom will have plenty of natural

light in the form of windows or skylights. Of course, you can use candle lighting for baths or a dimmer switch to allow for when you want more light in the room and when you want less. Since light kills many germs, especially in the bathroom, try to keep as much light in the room as comfortably possible.

COLOR

The best color choices for bathrooms are white and soft, warm tones in the honey beige family. If you want to use your bathroom as more of a peaceful escape, you should lean toward the warm earth tones like yellow and brown to minimize any negative energy.

If you have a clean, pristine white bathroom interior, you should decorate with hues of blue and green, since these colors will help you relax and your drainpipes to flow freely. Color psychologists agree that the color blue can actually reduce stress levels by lowering blood pressure, while green provides rest from eyestrain and has a calming effect similar to a soft, green field.

Some feng shui consultants will tell you that red is a good bathroom color for those who have difficulty waking up in the morning, but think about this powerful color carefully, since the bathroom is often the last room you are in before retiring to your bedroom at night. Red is a fire color, and while it can wake you in the morning, it can also keep you up for a restless night. Plus, the water elements in the bathroom will "put out" the fire element of red and its other incarnations in shape and object, making it less effective anyway.

Earth overpowers water, so using earth tones (and earthlike elements like faux marble) will keep the water from draining out—and keep your wealth in your family!

OTHER CONCERNS

What about tiles on the walls? These can be okay in terms of their reflective qualities (water), especially if you have a small bathroom that needs to be symbolically enlarged. But mirrored tiles are not a good idea in the bathroom, since these create a wealth-constricting effect that keeps the money contained rather than flowing.

However you decide to adorn your walls, do keep them clean. Hair can accumulate on walls, courtesy of the blow-dryer, and on floors, courtesy of the brush. Cleanliness is key to good feng shui in every room of the house, but especially in the bathroom.

MIRRORS

Feng shui consultants love mirrors for their reflective and space-enhancing magic. Just keep them useful and away from one another in larger bathrooms, since dueling mirrors can block energy. Mirrors that break up the image can split the energy they give off, so it's generally best to have a nice round mirror that is one brilliant piece.

If you don't have a round mirror, you can soften the hard edges of a square one by framing it or by having the glass cut in the corners to keep chi flowing and avoid poison arrows of sharp surfaces. Willow twigs in a clay jar next to the mirror will also help.

In feng shui, bathroom mirrors work best if they are simply flush with the wall, or function solely as mirrors. So, the protruding and multifunctional medicine chest can be less than ideal. It can still work in the feng shui bathroom as long as it is kept clean and clutter-free. The problem with many medicine chests is that they tend to become the storage bin for things that "might" get used someday (misplaced energy) or, worse yet, for things that are useless (stagnant chi). Hoarding things, even small items like makeup and tweezers, can block your prosperity by preventing new things from coming into your life.

Close the Lid

———

One of the things you'll hear every feng shui teacher say in a beginning class is that the toilet lid should always be closed to keep your wealth from going down the drain. This is a commonly held belief across all schools of feng shui: The toilet lid, if left up, will allow chi to drain away and take your money with it. So women have it right with their preference for the lid and seat down.

If the toilet can be seen from the entrance to the bathroom, you might consider using a small screen and keeping the door to the bathroom closed when not using it. If you can do it in a less-than-obvious way, conceal any water pipes that can otherwise be easily seen by you or your guests. You don't want to "see" your wealth slipping away, right?

Water should not be seen flowing away in the
form of a dripping sink faucet, tub, or shower stall.
In Chinese tradition, wasting water is wasting money,
because both are important resources.

For a toilet that is in the north corner, which pertains to business and career, you might place an earthen clay wind chime near it to keep the chi moving and to balance the water energy with an earth element. Such cures will keep your business success from going down the drain.

◀ If your toilet happens to be located in that tricky southeast corner of your home (the wealth corner), you can close the lid and keep a nice big stone on the toilet cover as a way of using an earth element to "ground" your finances.

If you want extra protection and chi activation, hang a small mirror on the outside of your bathroom door facing outward. The Chinese prefer a window in each bathroom for ventilation purposes, but if you don't have any windows in a bathroom, you can use mirrors in their place around the room and above the toilet.

One last word about toilets: If they are backed up, you will likely be backed up. Since the bathroom is in part an extension of your bodily "flow," you'll want it to be in the best working order possible at all times. You don't want it to overflow, keep running, or become blocked.

Creating a Relaxing Environment

Aside from being a place of cleanliness, your bathroom can be a sanctuary for relaxation and renewal. But how do you create a spa-like atmosphere and still follow the principles of good feng shui?

Just as you did with the kitchen, you need to appeal to all senses, mixing your own personal indulgences with the five elements in a balanced, yin-yang way that makes for a winning combination of nature and nurture.

THE PEACEFUL RETREAT

Creating a "no stress zone" in your bathroom can be done in a weekend—but if the thought of a complete overhaul creates more stress than it would seem to relieve, do it in small bits and pieces, one product at a time. Each time you add something new, it will feel like a new experience—one step closer to the new, totally balanced you!

Before you start to create a bathroom that offers peaceful retreat and restful relaxation, be sure to clear the clutter and clean the bathroom. You should also do a space clearing before every spa experience to maximize the health and well-being of your time alone.

Keeping the space clean and visually appealing will appeal to your sense of sight, as will good lighting and soft, curved shapes in your bathroom versus dark, angular areas.

Air the room out regularly by opening a window whenever you can, or by circulating the ceiling fan after each use of the bathroom. Fresh air is important to your health and also to the cleanliness of the bathroom. Opening the window also brings in a nice breeze while you are having your luxury bath—and simple, natural pleasures like this are truly wonderful and soothing.

SOOTHE THE SENSES

Set the mood with some quiet, meditative music. Whatever your musical preference, you should choose something that is reflective, soft, and uniquely you to appeal to your personal sense of sound.

Enhance smell in the bathroom easily by using bath oil beads, bubble bath, or potpourri. Here are some other suggestions:

- **Apply the basics of good aromatherapy.** If you are feeling depressed or anxious, use bergamot- or geranium-scented bath products; lavender is good for insomnia, and peppermint and orange bath products help boost energy. For particularly rough days, use bath products with a chamomile, lemon balm, or ylang-ylang smell. The scent of violets helps meditation. Scented milk bath products can also be soothing. Essential oils are available at most health food stores, and some can be used sparingly (if appropriate for bath use, and diluted first according to instructions) in a warm bathtub to enhance scent. Remember, it doesn't take more than a few drops!

- **Cleanse your body and your soul.** Mineral sea salts are the absolute best for a total cleansing, both inside and out. You can also use Epsom salts as a substitute. Dissolve the salts (about a pound of them; check product directions for guidelines) in warm bathwater; then sit back and relax for half an hour. You will be amazed at how good this will make you feel. There's a reason people have used sea salts for thousands of years! Always keep a few great bath bombs in a bowl nearby.

- **Use scented candles to enhance the senses of both smell and sight.** Candles offer wonderful aromas while being visually appealing—use colors that are significant to you. Be sure to use only pure and natural scents (with essential oils), as these are the strongest elements.

- **Inhale your scents, but don't forget to exhale them too.** Zen wisdom says that each breath draws in new energy, while each exhale cleanses the body of toxins. Remember this balance when you are meditating in your luxury bath—it's the best place for you to practice the meditative art of good breathing.

The sense of touch can be enhanced in the spa experience when you use bath oil beads (which soften the skin) or loofah scrubs (which loosen and remove dead skin). Removing dead skin is crucial to good feng shui care of the body, since dead things create stagnant chi. Try a fruit (like apricot) scrub once every two days or so to exfoliate; it really helps your skin feel fresh, smooth, and young if you make it part of a regular routine.

You can also massage the muscles on your face, neck, arms, legs, and feet while you are enjoying your spa bath. This will stimulate circulation, making your body tingle with rejuvenation. When you leave the "sacred space" of your tub, pat yourself dry with soft, fluffy towels in relaxing hues of blue and green. Don't forget moisturizer as a soothing finishing touch!

You also need to appeal to your sense of taste. Make yourself a fruit smoothie or a nice big glass of water with a lemon or lime twist. You'll want to replace the precious water that escaped your body via your pores. Fruit drinks are especially good; not only do they provide critical vitamins and minerals, but they restore the inner balance of your water element with fruit that is from the earth (earth element).

Chapter 8

The Bedroom

When you were small, you had trouble sleeping because there were monsters under your bed. Now, those monsters are in the clutter under your bed, atop your dresser, and in your closet. They are not the scary bed creatures from your childhood, but they prevent the flow of healing energy that can help you achieve a rewarding relationship, successful life, and good night's sleep.

Bedroom Basics

Unless you built your home from scratch, you obviously did not have anything to do with where your bedroom was placed. The decisions about which direction it faces and where it is in relation to other rooms or doors were out of your control. If, after you learn a bit more about ideal placement, these aspects begin to concern you, don't lose sleep over it! There is usually a remedy that will allow you to get a good night's sleep.

SLEEP TIGHT

Contrary to what many people think, a small bedroom is best—because the energy is contained—so long as the room is not filled with clutter. The best location for your room is far away from the front door of your home, where so much energy flows through.

Safety and privacy in your bedroom are important to restful sleep too. A bedroom that is too open to the rest of the house may be disquieting. If you must sleep in a space that otherwise lacks privacy, such as a living room, you should try to define the sleeping area clearly and protect it with a piece of furniture such as a bookcase or, perhaps, a tall screen.

If insomnia is a problem for you, "west is best" for the direction in which you should face, because that's where the sun sets. However, if you find it easy to fall asleep but difficult to wake up, try facing east. The direction of the sun, rising or setting, will help you determine what works best for you. Room color can help off-set too much or too little sunlight, as well.

TOSSING AND TURNING

If you fall asleep almost as soon as your head hits the pillow, you probably can move on to another section of this book. But if you're not finding a smooth transition from wakefulness to sleep, it could be because your bedroom feng shui needs some attention. The following checklist might help:

- The foot of your bed should not be facing the door—the so-called death position. Nor should your bed be parallel with the doorway. It should be positioned so that you can see the doorway, however.

- Eliminate mirrors. There are some exceptions to this rule, but, in general, mirrors displace the energy in your bedroom and impede astral travel—your soul's overnight adventures.

- Get rid of the clutter! Having remnants of your day, your work, and other aspects of your wakeful life scattered about your floor, hidden under your bed, and covering the surfaces of your dresser and any other furnishings impedes chi and your sleep.

- Try not to sleep directly under the bathroom on a floor above you. Being close to plumbing tends to drain chi.

- Have calm, soothing colors on your walls, floor, and furnishings.

- Keep electronics out of the bedroom as much as possible to avoid the constant flow of energetic electrical current while you're trying to sleep.

- Put only soft, comfortable sheets and blankets on your bed, and avoid using dead animal skins. No bearskin rugs on the floor! Dead animals in a room are very bad for chi.

- Keep your work area in another room, or cover it up when you sleep. Work and sleep just don't mix—and you don't want one of those frustrating dreams in which you're at work, only to wake up from your restless sleep and actually have to go there!

A WORD ON MIRRORS

Your bedroom should reflect your personal style, but mirrors should not reflect you—or you and your spouse or partner—in your bedroom. Mirrors displace the energy in your room, affecting your sleep, and even could draw other people into your romantic relationship. Mirrors over the bed are especially bad for that reason!

Also, not only might you be startled by your own movements in a mirror if you should get up in the middle of the night, but it's thought that each night, as we sleep, our souls travel through space and time. As they begin their journey, they also may be jarred by reflections in a mirror, including those of anything that is less than aesthetically pleasing in the room.

> The advantages of mirrors in interior decorating—opening up space and making a room appear larger and brighter—are serious disadvantages in the bedroom for those same reasons.

A mirror opposite the door of your bedroom is a bad idea too, because it will reflect energy back toward the entrance, interrupting the energy flow of your room. Exceptions to the no-mirrors rule are:

- If you cannot avoid having your back to the door, then a mirror on the opposite wall allows you to see anyone coming into your room. But use only one mirror, preferably circular, which facilitates a blending of energies.

- If your bed is directly under ceiling beams or a sloping ceiling, which disrupts or suppresses energy flow, then a mirror facing upward can help.

- If you want to reflect scenery from outside into your bedroom, a mirror can be used for that purpose.

- If you cannot simply remove the mirrors in your bedroom, you might consider covering them, such as with drapery or fabric art. If you do so, though, remember to use fabric of a muted shade, because bright colors are stimulating and can disturb your sleep.

Placing Your Bed

Where should your bed be? Let's first talk about where it should *not* be. Your bed should not be facing a doorway, with the foot of the bed toward the door. This is viewed as the death position in many cultures and is highly unlucky. Your bed should also not be aligned with the door, because you should be able to see anyone coming through the doorway. Also, this parallel position will create a disruption in energy flow that could disturb your sleep.

Placing your bed against a window is not a good idea either, since the chi will flow too quickly out of the room.

Another inauspicious location for a bed is under a beam, sloping ceiling, ceiling fan, bright light, or overhanging shelf or cupboard. All of these things disturb or suppress energy flow. Don't put your mattress on the floor, either, because that causes disturbed sleep and will hold you down from achieving your dreams. In your bedroom, you should seek to elevate yourself!

A few more caveats:

- If possible, you should not sleep on a bed that was owned by someone else, because beds absorb a person's energy, and chances are you do not know whether the energy of the previous owner was good.

- Don't sleep in a metal-framed bed. Not only is metal cold, but it will enhance the electromagnetic energy of electrical appliances in your home, which could prevent a restful night's sleep. Drape a metal frame with cloth to balance and soften its energy.

- Unplug as many of your electrical appliances in your room at night as you can to cut off the constant flow of electricity through the wiring.

- Don't sleep in a room directly below a toilet on the floor above, and if there is no door between your bedroom and bathroom, use something to separate the rooms. Bathrooms are believed to drain your energy.

- If you are a couple who values your relationship, it's recommended that you not sleep in a king-sized bed, which is too large and can have the same effect as sleeping separately.

- You should have a solid headboard (but not one shaped like a headstone). Use a canopy to separate your bed from what's over it if your bed is under a sloping ceiling, structural beam, or toilet on the floor above. Place the bed diagonally opposite the doorway to your bedroom, in a corner, so that you will see the door without directly facing it. Being able to see the doorway provides added security, which facilitates sleep. The idea is to be out of alignment with the energy flowing through the doorway while still keeping the doorway in sight.

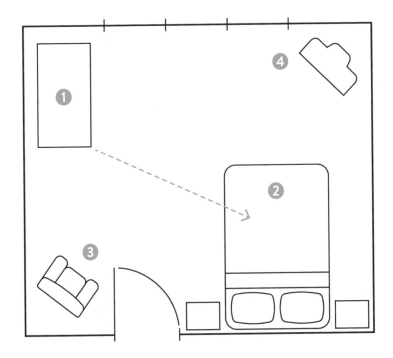

▲ A Less Than Ideal Arrangement: **1** The dresser (or bureau) is shooting poison arrows at the bed. **2** The bed itself is in a very vulnerable position, as the people in it cannot see much of anything, least of all the door. **3** The chair behind the door is probably not used for its intended purpose, but rather gathers discarded clothing, contributing to clutter and stagnant chi. **4** The TV is placed at a soft angle, which is okay, but it allows the TV to give off electrical energy, which can disturb sleep.

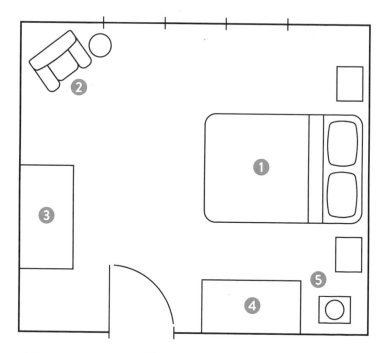

▲ A Better Arrangement: ❶ The bed's new location is much more auspicious, nestled between the children and relationships corners. It also has a view of the door. ❷ With the chair in the corner near a window, you may be more inclined to sit and read in it. ❸ Shelves, or an armoire, along that same wall (your knowledge/health areas) can hold your books, a plant, and even your TV (closing it off when it's not in use). ❹ The dresser is now in the helpful people corner—helping you stay organized and clutter-free. ❺ A mobile, or small piece of sculpture, in the corner next to the dresser will keep the chi from getting trapped next to the bed.

Eliminating Clutter

Many people have a tendency to allow their bedrooms to become filled with stuff. They rationalize that any guests who visit them will be highly unlikely to see their bedrooms, so why not throw all of those old boxes and magazines underneath the bed? It's that kind of thinking that can keep you up at night!

For the best possible energy flow and a good night's sleep, you really do want a room that is free of clutter. For instance, clothing that retains energy from your daily life should be put away. The space under your bed should be just that—space. There should be no storage boxes or fuzzy bedroom slippers, no snack food or dishes. No clutter of any kind. Also, except for the reasons previously noted, there should be no mirrors in your bedroom, and few, if any, knickknacks. No electrical appliances, including TV sets, radios, stereos, computers, or hair dryers. No exercise equipment, and absolutely no work desk!

If you must have a workspace (like a desk or computer) in your bedroom, just be sure to cover the work area at night. Hide your computer, for instance.

Try to reduce the amount of *things* you have, from the menagerie of glass animals to the jungle of real or artificial plants. In fact, living plants in your room at night are a bad idea, anyway. Nighttime is when plants give off carbon dioxide and take in oxygen, just the reverse of the process during the daytime.

Too many pictures on the walls, piles of books and magazines on the chairs and floor, and similar clutter will block the flow of natural energy and prevent you from achieving the best possible night's sleep. Even very large bedrooms should be sparsely furnished. Don't feel compelled to fill every inch of space, unless you truly enjoy insomnia.

Eliminating clutter doesn't mean you have to eliminate the things you enjoy. Instead of banishing books from your bedroom, for example, find a way to accommodate them and enhance the energy flow that induces sleep. Just place a pyramid-shaped bookcase in the wisdom corner of your bedroom. The books will be much more neatly arranged, and the shelf's pyramid shape works nicely, because it is an ancient symbol of higher knowledge.

Colors and Lighting

First and foremost, your bedroom is a place to rest your body, mind, and spirit. Be mindful of your decorative elements and their sensory impact. Calm colors, soothing fabrics, and subdued lighting will help you release the stresses of your day and prepare you for the sleep your body needs.

COLOR ME SLEEPY

Colors can do a lot to enhance your bedroom, but they can cause disturbance too. Be especially color conscious if you have difficulty sleeping. For instance, bright red is a great color for a fire engine, but not for your bedroom. Just as it startles and wakes up drivers and pedestrians, who rightly associate the color with emergencies and adrenaline, it will keep you awake at night.

Instead of using bright or glossy white, try a version of off-white, like eggshell or cream. Soft yellow, for instance, is considered an excellent color for a bedroom and is very conducive to a good night's rest. Gentle, warm colors, like some shades of pink, are exceptionally soothing. Who can stay awake for long while gazing at a soft nutmeg or soft, but rich, apricot color?

Very strong colors, including deep purple, red, and orange, are too strong for a relaxing bedroom. Green and turquoise blue are cool colors, better off in the bathroom or elsewhere in the home, and probably should be saved for accent, rather than serving as the dominant color scheme. Light green is preferable to dark green, and dark blue, similar to the color of deep bodies of water, should be avoided.

The same is true for patterns. Busy wallpaper and/or carpet will keep you buzzing all night long. Also, avoid the skins of dead animals in your bedroom, including sheep or leopard skin. Solid, soft colors, fabrics, and textures, preferably of natural materials, are your allies in winning a nice, long rest.

> Vivid colors of any hue will interfere with a restful night's sleep. Similarly, avoid the day-brightness of solid white; use it sparingly.

NIGHT LIGHTING

It's generally recommended that overhead lighting not be used in a bedroom, because of the intensity of light that will shine over your bed. Remember, too, that light is energy and therefore must be taken into account when the switch is on.

Even when the lights are off, however, the electrical current continues along its way, affecting the energy flow in your bedroom and, ultimately, your ability to sleep. Rather than an overhead light—and that includes overhead single or dual reading lamps that some bedrooms feature—try standing lamps or table lamps, off to the side, not shining over your bed.

Making sure you get a good night's rest isn't rocket science. All it takes is the same care, planning, and mindful attention to detail that you're using in all of the other areas of your home. The practice of feng shui in the bedroom is really the practice of creating the most restful, pleasing place to rejuvenate your body and soul. Make it a peaceful oasis!

Remember: It is generally best to keep computers and other electrical devices out of the bedroom if you want peaceful sleep. Electricity is forced energy; therefore, it can interfere with good sleep.

Room for Romance

Not all of your time in bed is spent sleeping, of course. And if you're very fortunate, you have a wonderful, loving partner with whom to explore the other possibilities. If you would like such a partner but do not presently have one, don't despair—feng shui can help you in the romance department too. All it takes is a little planning in your furniture purchases and arrangement, as well as your bedroom décor, and you can attract the relationship you most desire.

STARTING OVER

If you have recently ended a long-term relationship, and you can afford to do it, consider buying a new mattress. A bed, like other furnishings, absorbs the energy of the people who sleep in it, and you don't want any "old business" casting a shadow over your new relationship.

Throw away the holdover, sentimental pieces from your past relationship(s)—the theater or concert stubs and programs, old pictures, small gifts, souvenirs of trips together, and so on—but if you can't part with them altogether, at least keep them out of your relationship area so you can stay open for something new.

The end of a relationship is the perfect time for a clearing. Clear your space, certainly, but also consider freshening up or changing other elements of your bedroom. Your intentions will be personal, but they should also aim to change and improve the energy flow.

You want to attract a new person and a new way of relating to that person. After all, if your old habits were effective, you wouldn't be looking for someone new!

ART INSPIRES LIFE

In your bedroom, your artwork should depict happy, loving couples, not wistful-looking men or women sitting all alone. Nor is it a good idea to have pictures of lonely-looking, wave-battered cliffs, or isolated islands or rocks surrounded by a cold, blue sea and ominous gray skies.

You should have pairs of objects—for instance, a picture of a loving couple (or pair of birds), a pair of red candles, or two heart-shaped boxes—in your relationships area of the bagua, located in the rear right-hand corner of the room as you are looking into the room from the doorway. Some consultants suggest throwing sexy red lingerie or a silk robe into the corner and, in this particular area of the bedroom, hanging a round mirror to keep the energy moving.

Erotic art is appropriate in the bedroom, but refrain from displaying it in public areas of your house.

Be sure to keep your relationships corner clean—no dirty laundry, cobwebs, or dust bunnies. Red is the color of passion, and so some red in your relationships corner is desirable, even though you don't want that to be the color of your whole room. Symbols of romance and togetherness, such as hearts or a pair of doves or lovebirds, are ideal in that corner, especially since these birds mate for life.

Incorporating elements of feng shui works not only for attracting a new relationship but also for enhancing the one you have. Just keep your intention clear and positive, and don't place dried or wilted plants or flower arrangements in your relationships corner, since they represent death and decomposition (and you don't want these things to happen to your relationship!).

BUILD IT ANYWAY

Beyond your relationships corner, your entire bedroom should be set up for two. You should have two nightstands, one on either side of the bed, for instance, and a double or queen-sized bed, rather than a twin bed, which screams, "I'm still single!"

Make your bedroom appear welcoming to a special someone who might want to spend some time there with you. It should offer an obvious place for this person to put his or her clothing and other personal items without feeling too awkward about it. The room should, in other words, look like you were expecting company rather than building a private fortress or retreat.

Some lighter, brighter, more whimsical furnishings or decorative pieces are helpful too, because a loving relationship includes lightheartedness and fun. Avoid having a TV, computer, or workspace in your bedroom, because these will distract and detract from your relationship as well as disrupt the energy flow of your room. The only way around this in feng shui is to keep these electrical items tucked away in a small entertainment cabinet with cupboard doors that close when the item is not being used. To get the best sleep possible, be sure to turn all of these things off when you feel yourself nodding off.

THINK BALANCE

In keeping with the general advice about bedroom colors, take inventory of yours. Blues connote isolation, for instance. Warm earth colors, on the other hand, encourage closeness. In addition to having pairs of furnishings, you will want to achieve balance throughout the bedroom. Ideally, there should be a good balance of masculine and feminine décor to allow for a mix of yin and yang, which is ideal in all relationships.

Balance larger, heavier furnishings with some smaller, lighter ones. The arrangement of the bed and other furniture should be conducive to good energy flow, and mirrors, except maybe for that small round one in your relationships corner, should be avoided—especially over the bed.

Assess whether all areas of your room are open to the touch of another person, or are you still, in some way, holding back by guarding some precious items that you think of as being for you alone? Ideally, the person you hope to attract into your life, and your bedroom, will eventually add some touches of his or her own, but the attitude and energy established by you before that point are critical.

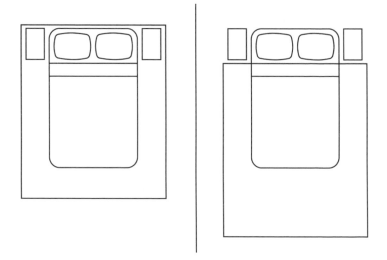

▲ Balance nightstands on each side of the bed. The foot of the bed should always be on the rug, even if the head of the bed is not.

A Sensual Experience

All right, so you never thought of your furniture arrangement as being especially sexy. But it can be—or, at least, *you* can be—once you have made the necessary adjustments to your bedroom. Sexual energy will be flowing like crazy then, and your only problem will be finding the time for all those partners who will want to get to know you a little better.

In general, it's best to have your bedroom in the back of the house and to pay close attention to what you place in your relationships corner, the rear right corner as you face the room from the doorway. Think red, hearts, candles, pairs of objects, pictures of happy couples, sexy lingerie, perfume, love poetry, and erotica. That's the corner that will help you turn the corner in your love life, so treat it well!

Mood music, aromatic candles, soft lighting, soft colors, and soft fabrics all contribute to a sexier bedroom as well. The art of seduction lies in soothing and sensual, not loud and brassy.

It also helps to relocate the family reunion from the bedroom to another room in the house. That is, remove pictures of your mom and dad, your kids, and your siblings from your bedroom walls. Who can feel sexy and uninhibited with those eyes on them? You might as well douse yourself with cold water and throw on some flannel!

If you want to have more love in your life, consider buying a pair of lovebirds and positioning them in the rear right-hand corner of your living room. What is more mindful than putting a pair of birds that mate for life in your relationships corner?

Chapter 9

The Kids' Rooms

You're exploring the role feng shui can play in your life. You're interested in putting its principles into practice. In your contemplative and mindful state, you walk past your child's room and are brought crashing down by a wall of chi. Are your kids' rooms a complete and total mess? Is there so much blocked chi in the room that it will take three hours to get them settled in for the night? Does the playroom look like an explosion went off? Not to worry. With a little creativity and cooperation you can help your children declutter and find balance in their personal spaces.

Clothing and Clutter

The two main problems (or opportunities, if you want to look at this in the Zen manner) with kids' rooms are clothing and clutter. Actually, these two are part of the same problem: an overabundance of all the things parents think children should have in order to have a fantastic childhood.

Take a good, hard look at the kind of example you're setting for your kids, and make regular assessments of the chi in all of the rooms they hang out in.

How do you know you have a problem with clutter in the kids' rooms? One sure sign is the telltale mountain of clothes that is piled on top of the dresser, with your child standing before it, unable to decide what to wear. When your child says, "I don't have anything to wear," what they really mean is, "I have too many things to wear and can't make a decision." Having too many options is very cumbersome, especially to smaller children who just aren't equipped to deal with those kinds of complicated choices yet.

First and foremost, as with any other room in feng shui, your kids' rooms need to be free of unnecessary clutter. Clutter (even too many clothes) can really disrupt the minds (and bodies) of your children, inhibiting their growth by holding down their energy.

Children really need only a few good outfits to wear—enough clothes for seven to ten days, maximum. Everything else will take up valuable space in the closets, until it begins to overflow and create monster piles everywhere else.

Feng shui dictates that all things, including children's clothes, should be acquired and used as they are needed, and never hoarded. Hoarding leads to blocked or buried chi; if you have too much stuff, inevitably some of it will never be used. Uselessness is not conducive to good chi, is it?

Getting Your Kids to Help

Okay, so *kids* and *cleanup* seem like mutually exclusive terms. But cleaner, neater kids' play areas and bedrooms *can* be achieved by using some of the same psychology you would use on a pack-rat roommate or spouse.

- Approach your child in a friendly, congenial manner and ask if he or she would like some help in putting things away. Sometimes, children—especially younger children—are reluctant to work alone because the task seems so overwhelming. But if you pitch in, even a little bit, the child's enthusiasm often grows. Be sure that you're not doing all the work, though. The lion's share should still be your child's!

- If you don't think your child uses or plays with some items anymore, don't just start putting them away or, worse, throwing them away or threatening to do so. Like anyone else, kids are fiercely protective of their things. Respect your child's need for some privacy and ownership.

- Try to get your child to see the logic in getting rid of unused items by asking some simple questions: "Is this still serving you? Does it bring you joy or have special meaning? If so, we can find a special place for it. If not, maybe we can donate it so that someone else can use it." Children often respond to the image of other, less fortunate, children who might derive some pleasure from the items that they, themselves, no longer use. Teach them to be good citizens of the world.

- Take the lead by becoming a positive example. When you clear your own clutter or "toys," you may inspire your children to do the same. Of course, items for donation must have all their parts and be in good working condition. You don't want to give your children the notion that it's all right to pass on unusable junk to charity.

- Create opportunities for storage solutions by placing a "collection container" in the child's playroom and/or bedroom. If there is a designated place for clutter collection, the clutter will become part of a more organized thought process—the first step in elimination! Colorful toy boxes with safety lids that can't shut on the child if he or she should try to hide inside them are ideal. Hampers work too.

You'll want to be positive, not punitive. Try to make cleanup less like punishment and more like fun. For example, start a race, with some small prize such as an extra bedtime story for the person who puts away the most items the fastest.

It is important that you not interfere too much with your child's process of getting rid of unused items, especially if the child seems reluctant. Inspire your child by setting a good example of a person who is free of the binding nature of "too many things." You don't want to be the "Do as I say, not as I do" parent; instead, you want to be a positive role model.

Be creative and have fun—that is the surest way to capture the interest and attention of your little wonders. Soon, you'll have them right there with you, putting down the toilet lids and hanging crystals all over the house. Make feng shui a positive activity full of learning opportunities, and you'll have happy, well-adjusted, and perfectly balanced kids!

BOOKS

One way to make sure the kids stay well balanced is to practice mindfulness and purpose in their rooms. Begin with making sure the bedroom is used for its rightful purpose, and that the activities of learning, sleeping, and healing are maximized.

Story time can be one of the best times to bond with your little miracles, but it can also be an enlightening experience for them if their books are stored in the best location for learning. Of course, the knowledge corner of the bagua is the ideal location for a small bookshelf full of tall tales and wonderful stories—but if that's where the bed is, then use this location to read stories that teach your kids something.

> The knowledge corner can also be a good place to position your child's desk, since it is there that your child will be likely to read lots of good learning materials (including the dreaded homework!).

In terms of storage, books for fun and creativity can be grouped and shelved right along with books for learning and growth. Where you can, try to use classic stories as a launchpad for mini-lessons on feng shui. For instance, you could talk about the three little pigs' trying to find a home with good chi, while trying to escape the bad chi of the big, bad wolf.

ELECTRONICS

If at all possible, designate a specific area of your home as an office/computer room, and keep the computers, TVs, and video games out of the bedroom. For example, consider an eight-year-old who could not relax enough to go to sleep at night. In the child's room, there were forty-eight movies stacked up next to a TV, and a PlayStation, Nintendo Switch, and Xbox connected to the TV as well! This electronic playground, coupled with scads of books, toys, and clothes piled everywhere, was the real reason the child couldn't unwind at bedtime. Really, who could with all that interference with chi?

In feng shui, electronics and electrical items are best kept away from the bedroom—their constant current can greatly interfere with sleep, and that's not a situation you want with growing kids. This includes cell phones, which tempt kids to stay up all night.

Ideally, kids' bedrooms are for sleeping and studying, and not for watching all-night TV when they should be in a peaceful dreamland that helps them grow and thrive. Remember, it is your spiritual duty as parents to teach your children how to create the spaces that will most benefit their growth, and rooms that serve their earthly purposes will always be the most auspicious gifts you can give them!

Using the Bagua

The bagua and its nine areas can be used in a child's room to create harmony, peace, and well-being, but you needn't get too worked up about making sure every single corner of the bagua is represented fully and completely in your child's room.

Luckily, only a few areas of the bagua need specific concentration. For example, it's highly unlikely that your two-year-old is looking for a love relationship beyond Mommy or Daddy, so you needn't go to too much trouble in the marriage/relationships corner.

Start instilling a respect for ancestors early on by including old photos of yourself as a baby or of other family members in the family section of the room's bagua. Such mindful efforts are especially auspicious if you include pictures or former belongings of a namesake.

The health area of the room is in the center, so be sure it's open and clear for the best chances of your child staying healthy year-round. When your child has an illness, you might consider hanging a healing crystal in the center of the room (out of reach). It may complement the wonders of a good antihistamine, without the drowsiness!

The knowledge corner, of course, is covered in the room's bagua by books or a study desk. If you use a night light (symbolic of fire, which corresponds to fame nicely) or even a mirror (if your child really wants to seem "bigger and stronger"), you will enhance the fame/reputation area too.

The main thing in using the bagua to enhance your child's room is to stay focused on the purpose of each corner—and think of creative ways to incorporate elements of each bagua section in as many corners of the room as you can.

If your child is afraid of the dark, use a flameless candle night light in a candleholder. Candles have calming energy. You can also purchase a plug-in night light that is red or that contains a picture of a fire element.

The Ideal Feng Shui Kids' Room

The most important thing you can do in your child's room is create a sense of belonging and balance. You want to encourage activity and creativity, but you also want your child to get rest for growth too. This yin-yang combination is a bit trickier to manage for children's rooms, but it is definitely not impossible! Keep moderating the energy as often as you can, and be sure to do regular space clearings in your kids' rooms.

In the ideal feng shui kids' room, the lighting is reflected up to the ceiling and bounces off of it much like strong tree energy that lets the sun in and out of the room.

Make sure you keep the storage boxes within safe reach for kids, and make them partners in keeping the toys where they belong by scheduling a nightly toy cleanup. Staying on top of the clutter on a daily basis will eliminate it for sure.

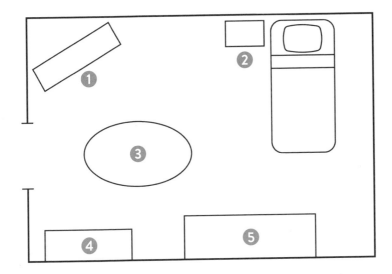

▲ Toys, books, and clothing should be stored neatly in boxes, or stacked in a closet (**4**), dresser (**5**), bookcase (**1**), or nightstand (**2**). They should not be left on the rug (**3**) or hidden under the bed, since stuff under the bed can lead to sleep disturbances.

Make feng shui a game with your children: Offer a reward to the child who can remove the most clutter. Enlist the help of your children throughout your process, and teach them a respect for chi or "life energy."

FENG SHUI FURNISHINGS

In the ideal bedroom for kids, the bed is placed in the room with the head facing north; if there are two beds, the beds are both facing the same direction to avoid trauma and sibling squabbles.

The beds are covered in soft, comfy cushions with a few pillows or stuffed animals tossed in for added critter comfort.

The furniture in the room is rounded or curved, with few, if any, sharp, pointy edges (poison arrows). If the children face east when they sit at activity tables or desks, their chi is heightened by the warm energy of the sun. Furniture in bright colors is very stimulating to the minds of children.

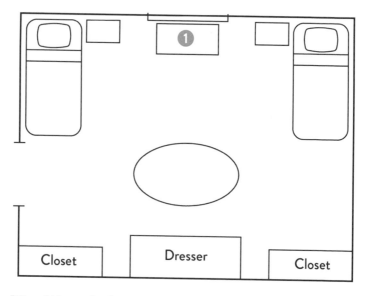

▲ When kids are sharing a room, always make sure that their beds are of equal size and facing the same direction (ideally north). Placing a bookshelf (❶) in between will encourage sharing of knowledge.

Remember: Window treatments (preferably fabric) slow
rushing chi and are especially good for rooms
with more than one window.

Floors are best left in the grounding energy of natural wood and can be softened by an area rug. If you want to add some interest to the room, you can do this with a brightly colored rug as opposed to a calming pastel.

COLORS

In the ideal feng shui kids' room, paint walls in harmonious, calming shades of blue and soft yellow. Consider hanging pictures of higher aspiration symbols (like mountains), or slow down the chi a bit with some fabric sculpture. Positive imagery should support and encourage your child to grow in a healthy manner.

Stimulate creativity by using bold color in unusual ways—perhaps hang a colorful picture of playing animals on a calm wall. Balance the calming yin colors (soft greens, pale blue, or yellow) with invigorating yang ones (bright orange, red, or primary blue)—with the exception of the hyperactive child's room. Here, you'll want to balance out your child's extreme yang with extreme yin—lots of soft, pale colors that help keep the mind from racing. In terms of the wall and overall décor of the room, a lot is going to depend on the age of your child, along with the child's personality and interests.

If your child is hyperactive (or extreme yang), paint the walls a calming shade of yellow, which is also good for study and quiet, introspective yin activities. Avoid reds and bright primary colors in the bedroom, as they keep the child active and disrupt sleep.

Speaking of interest, mobiles, safely out of reach, can make a terrific addition to any feng shui process in a child's room, since they really get the chi moving in all directions. The best part is that a mobile doesn't necessarily have to be for infants alone—there are plenty of interesting ones for older kids too!

For the younger set, the feng shui toy of choice is anything made of the wood element, since wood is strong and durable. But it's also earthy and nice to touch. Keep toys in plastic containers stored out of sight during sleep or study times.

LOCATION

You shouldn't locate the child's room in the center of the house or the back of the kitchen. Such locations are considered to be unfavorable in feng shui. A square or rectangular room works best for children. If two kids need to share a room, make sure they both have adequate and equal space, or there will be lots of arguments. Each child will also need to have something in the room that is uniquely his or hers in order to have a healthy spiritual attachment to the room.

Ideally, the best location for children's rooms is wherever there is sunlight. As flowers need sunlight to grow, so do children. Since the sunlight tends to come in through the east and southeast corners of your home, these are the best locations for your children's bedrooms. East is favorable because it is associated with the dawning of the new day and the beginning of new growth and development. This energy is really very invigorating and encouraging to children, who need the promise of a new day in which to grow.

The west is also good, especially for hyperactive children, because the sun comes into this area of your home later in the day.

The chi energy in the southeast is a bit more calming than the east, although it, too, promotes lively activity. If you want well-balanced kids who are neither hyperactive nor totally lethargic, look to the southeast for placement of the bedroom.

Western energy is quite settled and most auspicious for children who need lots of rest and a bedroom that is more of a peaceful retreat.

If you cannot have your child's room in any of these sections of your home, you can tone down the bossy chi of a northern room by hanging a mirror that sends the dominant energy of the room back to your own room—putting you back in control of the house, which, as parents, you should be. This simple feng shui cure will help you keep your rightful place as "the law" of the house.

> As a parent, you are your children's guide through life. It is your responsibility to help shape them, and to get them moving in the right direction in life. In essence, you are the director of their chi, since you help shape their lives.

YANG OPPORTUNITIES

The Chinese traditionally believe that the birth order of a child is what helps determine the child's potential for success in life—and that the room of a child should ideally have more yang influence than yin. In other words, the room should be full of life and potential, with mentally and visually enriching items.

Consider the following yang additions to a child's room:

- Posters or colorful pictures on the walls
- Bright or colorful painted walls
- Streamed music or CDs with plenty of learning-oriented stories and songs

Be careful of things like poison arrows (sharp lines), most often seen in the form of pointed shelves, study tables, or bedposts. Minimize harsh edges by draping soft cloth around them (as you might with a canopy bed), or deflect them by placing round or curved furniture (such as an inflatable or soft, rounded chair) nearby.

Things to avoid in a child's room: open doors, thick or heavy furniture, clutter under the beds (or anywhere else), headboards that are directly below windows, and electrical equipment that stays on constantly.

Speaking of poison arrows... Avoid sharp objects that depict any kind of war theme, including toys or pictures on the wall. To be able to sleep in peace, your children must also live in a peaceful room—that means no posters of video game assassins, or superheroes punching anyone out, and definitely no play guns hanging on the walls. Keep these kinds of toys stored away to keep their negative energy from interfering with your children's study or sleeping time.

ADDING THE ELEMENTS

When it comes to kids' rooms, don't forget the five elements of feng shui. Balance them in your children's rooms just as you would anywhere else in your home—except here you'll want to be a little more mindful of safety issues.

For instance, if you have a curious three- or four-year-old, you would not want to put a Zen fountain in your child's room. But if you have a preteen who has trouble concentrating on homework, a Zen fountain may be just the thing to help settle his or her nerves and maintain focus. The water element is good for reflection.

Organizing Playrooms

In your house, do you have a playroom that is disorganized and full of clutter? When you first assess the room, you will realize something you haven't before: In trying so hard to create an exciting life for your kids, what you were really doing was filling their lives with too much blocked energy. In essence, the amount of *stuff* that has accumulated may be holding them back from their true potential.

Your playroom should not become a dumping ground for all the toys in the house. Nor should it be completely sparse. A good balance in this room will include a small variety of stimulating toys, books, games, and movies to help your children expand their minds.

Remain mindful of the room's purpose, which is to entertain and stimulate your kids, not push them to overactivity and exhaustion, and you will have peace in your home.

If you have too much clutter in your playroom, why not donate some of it to a doctor's office for their waiting room, or to a women's shelter (where kids often stay as well)? Put the extra items to a healthier use in another space, and keep your own space for your kids' play area as open and inviting as possible.

Creating a Study Area

In China, education has a very high value in the lives of young children and their families. The Chinese believe that education is the only chance for their kids to escape poverty and move forward in their lives.

To create a study area that offers your kids the best opportunities for advancement in life, start with the furniture. Position the desk with the child angled toward and facing the doorway, rather than with his or her back to it. If you can't position the desk any other way and the child's back is to the door, hang a mirror so that the child isn't made to feel vulnerable. If your child is worried about who is coming up behind them, he or she may not be able to concentrate very well.

Set the example so that your kids know that feng shui can improve all of your lives. If you tell the kids they can't have a TV in their room, don't sit up late at night watching yours until you fall asleep.

The chair needs to be free and clear, without sharp points that can cause negative energy. Even posters, pictures, or book covers with angry or hostile scenes can cause study disturbances. Position a few pictures that symbolize higher aspirations, such as mountain scenes. Or hang a crystal (out of reach) over the desk to keep chi circulating and ideas flowing.

Don't place your child's desk so that it faces a window, since a window and all the outside activity will diminish your child's attention span. If you want greater concentration on studies, you can also place a Buddha on the desk for focus and meaning. If your child is a preteen who gives you attitude when you try to place a Buddha, you can always substitute a modern-day equivalent sage—why not try a Yoda figurine? Hey, if it keeps them focused, that's the point, right?

Ideally, your child should be able to study in one room and sleep in another. This is not always practical, so when study time has to be conducted in the bedroom, be sure to bring closure when it's time to shut the books and go to bed. Have your child place books in a book bag for school the next day and clear off the desk every night before turning out the lights. This will bring closure to the day's work and make you both feel ready and able to tackle the next day's offerings.

Creating a Sleep Area

When it comes to arranging and decorating infants' and young children's rooms, many of the "adult room" feng shui principles still apply. However, children are not adults, so, naturally, there are some big differences.

KEEP IT SIMPLE

It is not uncommon for parents—especially first-time parents—to overdecorate. Preparing for baby's arrival is fun and exciting, but try not to overdo it or concern yourself too much with interior design trends. For infants and small children, simplicity and muted colors, especially pastels and warm, gentle earth tones, plus soft textures in bedding and furnishings, are best for encouraging a restful state.

Try to avoid hanging too many mobiles or other exciting toys from the ceiling. Keep it simple—one or two calming ones positioned out of reach should do it. The rest of the house can wake up the child with brighter colors and a variety of textures, but the bedroom should, like yours, be quiet, peaceful, and calm in all ways. It's best to have interesting things, such as textures and toys, on the floor, where children can explore them when they are awake. Low furnishings with soft, rounded edges are best.

> Vibrant colors, wall hangings, designs, and toys will all keep the child awake and active and may even overstimulate him or her, leading to crankiness.

POSITION AND PLACEMENT

As with your room, the foot of the bed should not face the door to the room or be placed under a window. And it's best if the door to the child's room does not open directly onto the stair landing or face a bathroom. Try to avoid placing the child's bed under sloping ceilings, skylights, structural beams, and anything, such as a bookshelf, that might overhang the bed. Not only will items over the bed interrupt the chi, but they pose a safety hazard, as well.

READY FOR BED?

How do you best get your small children settled in for a quiet night's rest? Create a sensory experience that is conducive to good sleep:

1   For starters, make sure there is no clutter under the bed. Dim the lights and create a routine around relaxation. Set the mood with a soft night light and some meditative music.

2 Enhance your child's sleep patterns by remembering to turn off the music or any other electrical device after the child is asleep. This will minimize any possible interference with your child's sleep and allow the child to reach the deep state of sleep that is necessary for growth and rejuvenation.

3 If your child has lots of sleep disturbances, look for clues in his or her surroundings. Are the walls painted bright colors? Is there too much going on in the room? Are there too many pictures that depict action versus rest?

4 Double-check the direction the bed faces. If your child has a difficult time sleeping, move the bed so that its head faces either north or west—both directions are quite conducive to a good night's sleep. Northeast is not a good direction, especially for children, because its harsh energy can antagonize kids and cause more tantrums.

Think about what the room is saying to you, all the while asking yourself if this room is really promoting peace. If it's not, you'll need to make some changes. One of the most common changes you can make using feng shui principles is to paint the walls a soft, meditative color such as lavender or yellow, which are considered highly conducive to sleep.

Finally, don't forget to use other areas of your home to invite peaceful sleep to your children's rooms. For instance, you can practice some yoga or Zen breathing exercises in the living room before bedtime, followed by a trip to the bathroom for a warm, relaxing luxury bath.

Achieve good sleep for your children by taking lots of things into consideration and maximizing them for the intended purpose, which is sweet dreams!

Feng Shui for Older Children

The single biggest problem in most kids' and teenagers' rooms is clutter. Toys need containers. Children's rooms should be kept free of clutter, just like their parents' rooms, to permit better energy flow. Make cleanup fun with imaginative toy boxes, clothing hooks, and other kinds of organizers that are cheerful and whimsical, so kids will want to keep things neat, or at least will be a little less averse to the idea!

Furnishings that are sized appropriately for children, and that can be augmented or replaced as they grow, will help them feel comfortable and welcome in their own home. Make sure that they can see their door from their bed to heighten their sense of security. Furniture should have rounded edges and curving lines to avoid a feeling of rigidity as they grow.

Although bunk beds are practical, they are not good feng shui. The claustrophobic feeling of the lower bed, and the closeness to the ceiling of the upper bed, will stifle both occupants.

Remember to allow plenty of space for playing. Abstract art is beyond the comprehension of younger children, so provide art that is simple and that stimulates imagination. Storybook characters, or scenes of nature or the stars, will spark their creativity. Wall paintings can be a beautiful and comforting way of capturing a child's imagination or making him or her feel secure. Guardian angels or even protective animals such as friendly looking dogs help make children feel watched over. Encourage them to hang up their own art too!

Cupboards and bookshelves should be tall (and anchored securely to the wall), reflecting the growing child. Vertical stripes on drapes, linens, or other décor also enhance the feeling of growth.

Whenever possible, your children should have their own rooms, because they need privacy and the space to express themselves in their own living space, especially if they are more than a few years apart.

PERSONALIZE IT

Beyond the basic guidelines, nurture and accommodate your children's personalities in other specific ways.

- Less-energetic children, for instance, do better in larger, brighter rooms in which they can move around a bit, with some vibrant splashes of color on the walls, the bedding, or the furnishings to stimulate them.

- Physically active children, however, fare better in smaller bedrooms with quieter colors, where they cannot move around quite as freely. Especially helpful for these "type A" kids are construction toys, books, educational toys, and creative activities. Quiet games they can enjoy in their rooms will allow their minds and imaginations to come into play as well.

- Shy or anxious children are better off in rooms that feel secure, without rough edges or harsh lighting, and with soft fabrics, warm colors, and soft window treatments. The bed should be placed well away from the windows and the door, for better energy flow and a feeling of security.

- A small collection of stuffed animals (be mindful of clutter) and some soft music as part of the bedtime ritual provide security for all types of children. Remember to turn off the music system as soon as you know they are comfortably asleep, since you don't want the electrical "noise" to interfere with their dreams! As added protection against nightmares, hang Native American dream catchers in their rooms to ward off any scary apparitions.

THE TEEN CHALLENGE

Teenagers are a different feng shui beast altogether. Specifically, teens may favor darker hues like black in their rooms—the outward manifestation of their inward growth and introspection (remember how deep that time seemed?). These are years of metamorphosis, and so the self-absorption expressed by the color black should be accommodated in some way, if not on the walls, then perhaps in some of the furnishings.

Remember—with children of *any* age—to establish and monitor age-appropriate nonnegotiable ground rules regarding candles, incense, or any open flame. Setting a clear example yourself will help them establish safe habits that will last a long, healthy lifetime.

You may choose to accommodate your teen's preference by using black bedding, some black desk furniture, and some posters that are primarily black. Aromatic candles and incense contribute to self-awareness—if you are willing to allow your child to use them. Relative freedom to arrange or rearrange his or her living space is important to a teenager, who is on the verge of adulthood, even if the teenager's preferences do not conform to the rules of feng shui.

Room to Grow

In general, children's rooms will need to change and develop as they do. Rearranged furnishings, new furnishings, and different décor will all be desirable as they grow and their needs change. Children should be given the deciding vote in how their room will look (within reason). Although you probably will want to keep the walls, floors, and ceilings fairly calm to facilitate healthy sleep, allow your children some freedom in accessorizing through their bed linens, toys and toy containers, posters, and even some of their furnishings.

A little bit of autonomy will go a long way toward teaching children how to make decisions (a good skill for adulthood). They will also acquire a sense of taste all their own—equally important. The axiom about giving children both roots and wings is exemplified in how parents allow them to use their own private living space—an excellent dress rehearsal for their lives once they leave the nest. And you can always paint over their walls after they leave!

Books, toys, posters, and linens that are too young for your children, even if these things are in good condition, should be cleared out and replaced to allow the child to grow within as well as without.

In feng shui, it's often the empty spaces that tell the best stories about the future. In your kids' rooms, the open spaces tell the
story of your children's future: If the clutter is gone and there is
open space that allows the chi to flow in a positive way, your children will have the best opportunities for a healthy and lucky life.

As you look over the rooms of your children, be mindful of the
little miracles in life that you can create for them just by opening
up their space and balancing the chi—and remember that you're
teaching them how to create their own opportunities for miracles
in life too.

Chapter 10

Your Business

Although it's been around for thousands of years and has been used in Asian businesses for centuries, the art of feng shui has only recently found its place of honor in Western business. In a corporate office setting, good flow of energy is essential to worker productivity—and company profitability. Creating an open workspace can also alleviate stress, another productivity zapper. This chapter will help you incorporate the practices of feng shui into your business, company office, or home office for maximum productivity.

Finding the Perfect Location

When you're checking out a new business location, you'll have a lot to consider. It's more than just looking at high-traffic areas or commerce centers; it's looking into the history and the lay of the land.

THE NATURAL LANDSCAPE

Landscape design is important to the success of your business. According to many feng shui consultants, the most auspicious lots are circular or horseshoe shaped and are located near the base of a hill with elevated land on either side. Although this positioning is protective and good for home locations, if your office or business is located at the foot of a large hill, you can expect to be fighting uphill battles in keeping the business afloat year to year—at least according to Chinese tradition.

Although roads that lead directly into your business are not considered good in feng shui, they might work well for drive-through businesses, which are designed with rushing chi in mind.

If you can help it, try not to locate your business too close to any one particular element (especially an ocean). Facing a smaller body of water such as a pond would be a fortunate position for your business, as would a position in which you are looking down on a steady, flowing body of water (but not a fast-flowing stream, which symbolizes rushing chi). Roads in feng shui are much like rivers or streams and should, ideally, meander around your business rather than draw people directly into it.

THE NEIGHBORHOOD

Look for poison arrows (sharp corners) near your proposed business site before signing on the dotted line. If there are lots of poison arrows, you can still lease or purchase the site, just be sure to hire a feng shui consultant to install some necessary cures (such as a mirror that reflects the poison arrow back to its owner and away from your building, or even a metal wind chime to dissipate the negative chi). In terms of the shapes of neighboring buildings, the rooftops should ideally be varied in their height rather than all one level; such variations will help each business in the immediate vicinity maintain its unique identity.

If you use a mirror in your business or office, be sure it doesn't reflect the "sha" or negative chi of a bathroom or staircase.

If you are considering a location that is older and has been occupied previously by other businesses, be sure to run a little background check on the site. If the previous business didn't do well, try to find out why. Address those issues first by doing a good space clearing, and then by paying particular attention to the wealth section of the business's bagua. Add extra wealth cures to this corner of your business to increase its chances of success over its predecessor's.

The Lobby

———

Once inside, your visitors should feel welcomed and embraced by your business. It's best if your entrance faces an open area with lots of bright light, and the entry doors should be large enough to accommodate the chi moving into and out of your business each day.

Reception areas also need to be located in open, well-lit places to encourage good chi. But if the area is too open, it could allow visitors to pass by too quickly, leading to security problems. A divider would help in this situation. Conversely, your reception area shouldn't be unwelcoming, with several straight-lined cubicles and pathways that force visitors to go through a maze of workstations before they find anyone who can help them. This is very negative chi for a business, since your competitive edge can hinge on customer service and responsiveness.

———

Lost souls meandering around your office looking for a person to help them find their way is not conducive to repeat business—and many people might not try that hard even the first time. *That* is bad feng shui.

———

For added flow of chi in the reception area, stagger the workstations, use screens with soft fabrics rather than large cubicle walls, or place a water fountain in the wealth corner of the reception. Not only do these cures seem more welcoming, but they will contribute greatly to your team's productivity, resulting in a better bottom line and lots of happy customers. Who could want more than that in business?

The Cubicles

Let's face it, cubicles are a way of life for those who work in the corporate world. While some people enjoy the den-like security of working in a small space, others wish for a workspace all their own, a place in which they can work uninterrupted on a project, and even kick the door shut for a conference or two. Of course, the reality is that there are often too many workers sharing too small a space, leading to the necessary construction of cubicles.

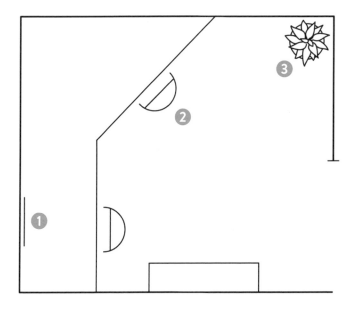

▲ Use a mirror (❶) if your back is to your cubicle's entrance. Place a plant (❸) or hang chimes directly across from the entrance to slow down chi. Place any additional seating (❷) diagonally across from the entrance to encourage honest conversation.

"Cubes" don't have to be confining spaces, however, especially in terms of creativity. It's all in how you approach your surroundings, and the quality of the intention behind your décor. So many cubicles are left stark by inhabitants who have never gone beyond hanging a memo on the wall, let alone given thought to placing a plant, a mirror, or anything that employs the principles of feng shui. Don't be bland; show some life and know that when you "claim" a space, you can improve your work attitude, which could also have the added bonus of helping you keep your job or even be promoted later on.

Here are some tips for surviving life in the cubes:

WATCH YOUR BACK

Always be sure you can see who is coming up behind you. Unfortunately, most cubicles are designed in the weakest feng shui position there is, forcing your back to its entrance. So, you'll need to devise a way for yourself to keep from being surprised. You will want to place a small mirror at an angle that will allow you to see behind you. An eye on your cubicle entrance keeps you from feeling vulnerable to potential backstabbers or even well-meaning people who could otherwise make you jump out of your chair by seeming to sneak up on you.

DEALING WITH THE OPEN WORKSPACE

If you are working in an open space (with no separating cubicle walls), try your best to face the office doorway. If this is not possible, you'll need to place a mirror on your desk to reflect the mouth of chi in the workspace. To soothe the stress of working in a "fishbowl," you might consider listening to calming music with water sounds while you work, or placing a photo of a waterfall or ocean scene on your desk or as your screen saver. Keep the clutter in check and include a living plant for positive, nurturing energy.

DON'T FORGET THE DOOR

Make sure that you can always see an entrance. If you can't see one from where you sit, suggest to the office manager that they purchase a mirror to position on the nearest corner wall, so everyone can see who's coming into an office and who's leaving. Not only is such an addition good feng shui, but it's becoming increasingly necessary in these days of heightened office security due to the unfortunate risk of workplace violence.

Take it personally! Make your space as homelike as possible. You'll want your cubicle to feel comfortable and welcoming to you each day when you arrive at work.

PROTECTIVE WALLS

If you are in direct line with a door, create a barrier. Being in the line of fire, so to speak, will keep you always on the defensive. The lack of privacy is bound to make you feel like you're always being watched. You could do something as simple as placing a plant near the entrance of your cubicle, or even perhaps create a small screen using drapery or beads. Of course, you'll need to comply with office policy here, but there are ways around every negative situation using the Black Hat Sect of feng shui. Be solution minded! (Note: If you have a particularly nosy boss, hang a piece of stained glass with an all-seeing eye on it—your boss will get the message.)

Cubicles don't need to be oppressive, uncreative workspaces. Although they can present design and décor challenges, from a feng shui standpoint, there is nothing that cannot be corrected using cures such as small aquariums, plants, or even hanging crystals. Be sure to update your surroundings when anything about your job or the company changes (like your title due to a promotion, a colleague's departure, or a new company name as a result of a merger). Do a space clearing each time!

Enhancing Chi in the Workplace

You already know that a harmonious workplace is a productive one, but what's the best way to achieve good chi in your work environment? Actually, there are several things you can do to enhance chi and increase the sense of harmony and well-being in your office:

- **Keep up with cleanliness and clutter removal.** Don't be a clutter junkie. Hanging on to old memos, files, and messages will only hold you to the past and keep you from moving toward the future. If you work in a field where archiving is required, designate a particular place in the office for a library. Deal with your paper trails efficiently and you'll never be left behind in the corporate dust.

- **Live in harmony with your mechanical equipment.** Fighting with inanimate objects such as computers is not good feng shui. Appreciate the items that are useful to you by showing them respect and reverence. By being good to your cell phone, tablet or computer, you will help it serve you better! (P.S. Don't clutter your phone with too many useless apps!)

- **Live in harmony with coworkers.** Keep gossip and negativity out of your work life, because what goes around, comes around. Try to stay positive every day.

- **Shed some light on important matters.** Most often, offices don't lend themselves to high-quality natural lighting. Improvise by buying a good desk lamp with natural, full-spectrum light bulbs. Such a minor change will give you the maximum amount of healthy light and will even work to improve your mood if you happen to suffer from seasonal affective disorder.

The biggest changes you can make to improve your work experience really come from within. Taking a mindful approach to your peers and your environment will improve both your attitude and your performance. Not only will you do (and feel) much better, but the good chi, and good spirits, you bring to the office will benefit everyone!

Feng Shui in Meetings

Most companies' important business happens in meeting rooms or boardrooms, so pay attention to those rooms as well. In addition to the major aspects of your conference rooms (which can vary depending on their purpose), certain other elements are fast and simple. Consider implementing the following:

- To encourage creativity in a brainstorming meeting, try hanging a crystal in the children/creativity corner of the boardroom's bagua to activate chi and stimulate creative thought.

- For a top-level discussion about the company's financial standing, you should focus on the wealth corner. Use a small water fountain during the meeting or place a picture of a waterfall there.

- Reduce interfering chi by using a room that doesn't have too many doors or windows, since both can lead to distraction, disruption, or even quarrels.

Since the boardroom is where all the action begins and ends, you'll want to do regular space clearings in this chi-filled room, especially after any major changes. You'll need to clear the energy after any negative outbursts, too, since you won't want the negative energy of argument to linger (or spill into the next meeting). Even a simple handclap can disperse bad energy.

Yellow in your office can stimulate intellectual ability, creativity, and thought. It also promotes self-discipline and follow-through, both good qualities for an employee or executive.

CORNER OFFICE, CORNER SEAT

The president, manager, or leader should always be in the position of greatest strength at the table—most often, that's the corner facing southeast (beneficial for leadership and authority). Let each person who arrives at the table after the leader assume a position that is most comfortable for him or her. Most often, attendees will gravitate toward the spot on the table's bagua that corresponds to what they most need to focus on. For instance, a timid person may instinctively choose to sit in the southeast corner since it is farthest away from the leader. This is okay because the northwest corner of the table represents communication, dignity, and respect—all things the timid worker is no doubt focusing on as areas of self-improvement. Not everyone can be a leader and sit facing the southeast corner!

SET SOME PROTECTIONS

If avoiding a hostile takeover is part of the meeting's agenda, you can anchor the protective elements in the room by placing potted trees in each corner—carry this through the entire office if you want. That's not a guarantee that another company won't acquire yours, but it can go a long way in protecting your collective psyche. It will also help keep morale high despite the financial climate. You don't have to believe in every single aspect of feng shui for it to have a beneficial effect.

Using Feng Shui in Your Brand

Your business identity extends way beyond the lobby and the boardroom of your office. You display it to the whole world in the form of your logo, business card, letterhead, and website. So often, especially with entrepreneurial start-ups, such identity items are an afterthought, when, combining good feng shui and business principles, they actually should come first.

Be mindful in knowing yourself and your business, then consider how you want to be seen and known for what you do. How else can you build a strong brand around your business except with a logo and its unified business identity pieces (including advertising, along with the company letterhead, social media presence, automated marketing, business cards, and website)?

MORE MINDFUL DESIGN

Your business card, which will be seen every day by people considering doing business with your company, can utilize feng shui for its most auspicious impact—starting with the dimensions you choose. Feng shui consultant Lillian Too uses a business card that is 2 inches in both width and length, which she considers the most auspicious dimensions for abundance and wealth. It must be working, since she is one of the most popular feng shui consultants in the world!

Logo designs that contain lots of sharp, pointed, or angular parts are generally not considered to be auspicious for business, since they, in effect, shoot poison arrows at your business (or, worse yet, at potential clients!). Use harmonious color combinations like black with white, green, and metallic colors, or brown with blue.

Black and red, red and orange, and black and yellow are all considered to be inauspicious business card or logo color combinations. Use harmonious colors instead.

Pay attention to the balance and feel of your logo and business card design. If it's too busy, with lots of color, artwork, and words, you're bound to look scattered and unprofessional. If it's too sparse and uninteresting, you'll look like you aren't sure of yourself. Take the moderate approach and strategically place the elements on your business card, from the logo art to correct wording. If you're not sure what balance and symmetry are, hire a graphic designer to produce your business cards so they have the best chance of creating a positive picture in the minds of their recipients.

YOUR WEBSITE

In terms of web-savvy feng shui, design your website with the flow of chi in mind. After all, you want your prospective customers to be able to navigate freely and without experiencing any blockages, right? Maximize the use of your links to ensure a smooth, flowing experience from one page of your site to the next—as seamlessly as possible.

Purple is a wealth color, but it is also a power color that will help separate you from your competition. Use it in your logo or on your desk—and don't forget to add some "power colors" to your computer screen.

In terms of color online, use bright colors balanced with white for a crisp, attractive look. Bold colors can activate chi for your website, as can any kind of animated images. Use animation judiciously, however, since you won't want to overstimulate viewers with too much action—and with chi that seems to be rushing all around with animated graphics or lots of links leading from your site to other places.

Use mindfulness and intention to move your prospects from one area of your site to another, without sending them away until they reach the end of your site (that's why so many links pages are the last button to click on a page). Stimulate the chi of each person who visits your site by leading him or her through the process of viewing, page by page and image by image. Create an experience. Go for nice, crisp, bold images used sparingly on a page with some focused, interesting content. Too many images and too little content tells your customer that the company is more interested in the aesthetics of creating an image than in educating people about their intent. Why does your company exist? Whom does it serve, and how is this accomplished? Make it easy for people to do business with you by taking the time to design your site with feng shui in mind.

A web page is a sales tool for reaching the broadest possible audience. With that in mind, remember that for salespeople, red is a wonderful color: It is powerful and aggressive, and it relates to the fame (and reputation!) sector of the bagua.

There are plenty of other things to take into consideration with your feng shui website. Here are other auspicious elements for the "well connected" website:

- **Simplicity.** Keeping your site simple and uncluttered is in step with one of the main principles of feng shui: Eliminate clutter. Also, use all space well in your web design; don't box in the chi by lining all of your components against the four sides of the screen. Choose only the best links to include on your site; don't clutter pages with long lists of links just to look impressive.

- **Yin and yang.** On the well-balanced site, movement counteracts the many straight and angular lines or sharp corners produced by some designs (or the computer screen itself), but there is also a stillness that allows the eye to focus on a particular area that feels grounded. Your logo, for example, could appear in the same area of every page on your site, or your navigational images could be consistent from one page to the next. Revamp sites with lots of straight lines to include some wavy or meandering lines to achieve balance (not to mention add great interest!). Think in terms of opposites to keep your site well balanced.

- **Direction.** Ideally, your site will be intuitively easy for viewers to navigate smoothly. If they feel backed into a corner on a page where they cannot move either forward or backward within your site, not only have you lost their interest on the page, but you've also probably lost them as potential customers. Customers expect easy-to-navigate sites. Using the principles of good feng shui, you should have no problem getting customers to where they want to be—both on your site and in their lives.

- **Appeal.** Your splash page or home page should be warm, interesting, and inviting. It can also be bold, as long as you limit the amount of color and animation on the page. In feng shui terms, the home page is the mouth of chi on the web. If customers can't make it through the mouth, they'll never venture further than your symbolic front door.

- **Harmony.** Good harmony on your website, in the feng shui sense, means creating a pleasant experience—aligning yourself with harmonious relationships. You should evaluate every relationship that is key to the development, hosting, and marketing of your site. Web designers or ISPs (Internet service providers) with a bad track record are not harmonious folks to include in the development of your site. Think carefully about whom you align yourself with, even in the links you provide to other businesses. In business, your reputation is very important and often hinges on whom you are associated with and why.

The yin and the yang of websites is to keep them uncluttered yet powerfully attractive, focused yet interesting, and open-ended yet well directed. Apply feng shui and you will be happy with the results!

Feng Shui for Work Advancement

You've applied feng shui to your tiny cubicle and meeting rooms, and even helped improve the lobby of your company. Now, how can feng shui help you climb the corporate ladder?

FACE-FIRST

Make sure you have plenty of flowing energy all around you, and that you are facing the right direction. For fame and recognition in your field, you'll want to be facing the fame section of the bagua, which would be the south wall. If you can't sit facing this direction, try placing a fiery red object (painting, flowerpot, small sculpture) in this area of your office.

If you are feeling sluggish at your desk, infuse a little energy in the form of the color red. Red is an energizing color, and since it represents the fire element, it is sure to "light a fire" under you to get you motivated!

For career advancement, try facing north so that you are activating the career section of your office bagua. If you want, you can move your computer to this area (as long as you can still see the doorway clearly) or place certificates of recognition there to show your "worth." To enhance working relationships, use the southwest corner, since it represents the relationships area of your bagua. Pictures of people shaking hands or conducting positive business deals together are good here, as are quotes about teamwork.

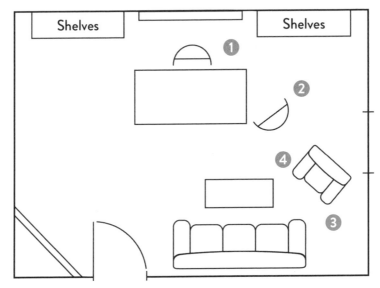

▲ This plan works for most offices because it is relatively simple. ❶ From behind your desk, you can see the door, yet you are not directly facing it. ❷ The desk's guest chair is placed in the desk's (not the office's) wealth/health segments, encouraging visitors who will feed the health and wealth of your business. ❸ The office also has a more casual seating area in its helpful people corner, for more intimate and comfortable conversations. ❹ Note that the single armchair still has a good view of the door.

DRESS YOUR DESK

Square or rectangular desks are better for making more money; round or oval ones enhance creativity (which can get you promoted). The darker the desk, the harder it will be to get work done.

Use the bagua on your desk to its fullest advantage: Put your planner in the northwest (helpful people/travel) corner of your office desk (which is a different placement than on your home desk), family photos in the family section, and whatever you most want to achieve in your fame section (i.e., a new car, a picture of someone doing the kind of work you want to do, or any other image meaningful to you with regard to your future—just use the rear center of the desk). For added chi activation, hang a crystal in your fame/recognition corner too.

PUT YOUR BEST FOOT FORWARD

If you're making a career-advancing presentation, try to place your body in the most auspicious direction you can (i.e., in the relationships corner for a people-oriented presentation, or in the fame corner for your chance to shine in the spotlight). If it feels like the right position for you, it probably is.

WORK FROM GOOD INTENTIONS

Remember the golden rule of the universe (also known as the universal law of attraction): What you put out there is what you are likely to get back. If you are constantly spreading rumors and negative things about the company or your coworkers, you can expect the universe to keep throwing it back at you. Positive people get what they want; all they have to do is put positive intention out there and spread the good chi. There is enough good chi for everyone, and the more you give, the more you are likely to receive in the way of goodness, recognition, and abundance.

Creating a successful company or career can be easy using feng shui—just don't get too hung up on the details. Trust your intuition. Learn to go with the flow. You can do it!

Business Pointers

Be mindful of the following useful tips when using feng shui to achieve your career goals:

- Location, appearance, and the history of your place of business are critical. Landscape design, surrounding elements (such as roads or bodies of water), sharp corners on the site, the shape and height of nearby buildings, as well as the history of other businesses that may have occupied your building all play a role in the success of your business.

- The lobby should be warm, welcoming, bright, and airy, as should the reception areas. These spaces should not be too open, however, or visitors may pass by too quickly.

- Cubicles should be welcoming and should reflect as much of the occupant's personal tastes as possible. Plants or feng shui articles like mirrors and crystals can help instill life and increase energy flow in the space. Make your cubicle feel a bit homelike, if you can.

- Even in a cubicle, try to arrange things so you can see who is coming up behind you—say, by using a mirror. You may also need a mirror to help you see the entrance of the office.

- Create a barrier if you are in direct line with a door to prevent you always being on the defensive; the lack of privacy is also bound to bother you. Try placing a plant near the entrance of your cubicle, or even perhaps create a small screen using drapery or beads.

- Keep up with cleanliness and clutter removal. Retaining old files and messages will only hold you back and prevent your moving forward.

- Cooperate harmoniously with coworkers. Keep gossip and negativity out of your work life and you will become a conduit of good.

- Consider direction, not only for office furnishings but for yourself. If you're making a presentation that is critical to your advancement, for instance, try placing your body in the most favorable direction you can.

- In general, career advancement using the principles of feng shui has to do with sending positive energy into the universe so that it will come back to you. Work in accordance with the universal law of attraction: What you put out is what you are likely to receive.

Your Home Office

If you run a business out of your home, you've probably already devoted a lot of attention to your business plan and everything affected by it, but more than likely you haven't given as much thought to the basics of your office layout. Or maybe you haven't even chosen the space for your office yet and are experiencing excess clutter on your kitchen or dining room table.

Although many great businesses have gotten their start at those tables, very few are successful if they are held back by the negative energy of clutter and misguided intention. In good feng shui, you must be as mindful of the way you treat your business as you are mindful of its proper guidance and growth into the future. Don't bog down your dreams by confining them to a space that's really intended for eating, or your dreams will indeed be washed down the drain with yesterday's leftovers!

In a few easy steps, you can put together a home office that supports and enhances your dreams, rather than suppresses them. Review and consider each step so you can start your home business moving in the right—and most auspicious—direction.

It's best to have more energy in front of your desk than behind it, if you want more business to come to you.

DETERMINE THE BEST WORKSPACE

Take a good, hard look at the kind of work you will be doing in your home office. Will you be conducting high-powered sales deals or low-key writing assignments? Will there be clients coming to your home office, or will you have the kind of privacy that enables you to literally work in your pajamas? An assessment of the kind of energy *you* will be expending in this space can go a long way toward helping you choose the best location for it. In feng shui, everything begins with energy!

Place symbols of success or a list of goals in the fame/ reputation corner of your home office to help you be mindful of old successes while visualizing new ones.

Once you've given thought to the kind of work you'll be doing in your home office, you can start thinking about how you would best like to accomplish it. The idea here is to create a workspace that is in harmony, or in flow, with your life and your goals. Do you want to make a comfortable living in your current line of business, or do you want to shoot for the stars and become a millionaire?

Every dream starts with a goal, and every feng shui assessment begins with a look at your goals to determine whether each room truly supports those goals.

Which room works best for a home office? Well, it depends. If you've got a den, that's great, because it is space especially designed to accommodate a home office. Easily accomplished, right? Think about where the den is in relation to the bagua: Is it located in your wealth sector? Great! If it isn't, does this mean you won't be successful? Hardly. It just means you'll need to spend more time positioning your business for its best chances of success. That requires some planning, but more than anything else, it requires mindfulness about what you want in your life and what you don't want.

Consider the possible shape of your home office. Rectangular works best from a feng shui standpoint, since it allows the chi to flow freely as long as it is not interrupted by furniture. L-shaped offices can work too, but be careful not to position yourself in a sharp-edged corner of the space. Beware of sharp edges, since they cut chi in a room. You can soften sharp lines and edges by adding a soft element such as a red fabric cord (which can be hung from the ceiling in front of a sharp corner) or draped fabric (in front of the spot where two sharp lines meet).

If your only available space is in your bedroom, then create a small workspace using a small desk that has cabinets that close, or employ some other item (such as an expandable screen) that hides or covers your equipment when you're not using it.

You can have your office in unusual places throughout your home, as long as you don't disrupt the flow of positive energy in your workspace. Many people have outside structures such as a converted garage or small cottage that they use as a home office, and this can also be good feng shui. Try to keep your work life and home life as separate as you can, though, and you will find that your home business brings invigorating new energy to your home without causing a major disruption to your family's life.

A room that is located toward the front of your home is considered in feng shui to be an auspicious or fortunate location, since chi flows in from the front of the house and has a more difficult time reaching the back. Good chi is especially important when you meet clients at your home office.

Before you start moving your office furniture around, you should do everything you can to start with a clean slate in your home office. That means, "Clean up the clutter!"

SET THE STAGE FOR SUCCESS

You've cleaned up your clutter and cleared your space—now what do you do to have a remote workspace or home office that uses principles of good feng shui? You position your office furnishings in a way that increases your potential for success!

- Curved, round, or oval desks work best for keeping chi open (especially important for creative types such as writers and graphic designers). Wooden desks activate natural chi, since wood is one of the natural elements used in feng shui.

- Be sure your desk is in the wealth corner and your back is not to a door. A desk can be angled in the wealth corner if there are two doors in the room.

- Facing a window can inspire you, but being surrounded by them can actually inhibit creativity. Too many windows in your home office can be distracting, so use some draperies or mini-blinds to control the amount of chi lost through such a space.

- Keep a crystal bowl, plant, or small water fountain in the wealth corner of your desk or home office. These objects tend to attract or increase prosperity. An expensive, beautiful object of art will work the same way.

- Place a deep-blue rug in the middle of the room—it represents the water element and will give you the feeling of gazing into the water for reflective moments or times when you need to meditate over a business decision.

- Bright red objects in the rear left (wealth) corner of your home office can increase the financial success of your home-based business. Use a picture of red flowers, a red cord, or red silk in this area for good money luck.

- No place for indoor plants? Don't have a green thumb? Instead of torturing yourself, use pictures of plants in areas where you seek vibrant good health and well-being.

- Use a hanging crystal or wind chime in your fame and reputation corner. Don't use anything that's blue in color in that corner, since blue represents water. Water in the fame quadrant of the bagua can literally drown it out.

- Place only objects that are useful or meaningful to you (and your business!) in your office. The key to home office success is creating a space where you will feel whole, inspired, comfortable, and energized. Too much clutter inhibits creativity.

- If you don't have any windows in your home office, use lots of bright color in your décor. Hang unusual, interesting, and brightly colored objects on the walls wherever you can, but remember that the placement of a few nice larger items is always better than lots of little ones.

- Safely cover electrical wires to minimize electrical disturbance. Electricity can create a thick energy that bogs you down.

- Decorate your office in calming colors such as lavender, soft pink, or light shades of blue.

- To lessen feelings of chaos, eliminate clutter (a major and recurring problem in feng shui) and ground swirling energy with a fountain or Zen garden that will help slow your mind down.

- To feel a connection to the main office (if applicable), include an object of corporate meaning to a remote workspace. For instance, hang a company calendar in the helpful people corner.

Remember: Every item carries an energy with it;
be sure it's an energy you really want to use before
you put something new on your desk.

The principles of feng shui are not only related to style and placement of your furniture and objects. Be as mindful in managing your office as you are in keeping your home. Clean computer files regularly (including cache files and hard drives), and keep one centralized planner (print or electronic) with a place to list your professional and personal commitments and goals, placing it in your helpful people/travel corner. Keep both your physical surroundings and filing/business systems as streamlined as possible.

COLOR BY TYPE
Creative types perform their specialized tasks very well in soothing tones of blue-green. These colors will work well to soothe

you when you feel like your mind is running overtime with creative ideas. Blue-green is reflective and helps slow down rushing thoughts. Conversely, purple can stimulate creative activity when you feel you are in a creative slump.

Red can frighten creative types by its boldness, but sales and marketing folks find it invigorating because it represents aggressiveness in the business setting. If you're working on the edge as a sales pro, stockbroker, or manufacturer's rep, red can be an auspicious color to use in your home office. You needn't paint every wall red for it to be effective, either. Sometimes, all you need to do is add a splash of bold color.

Aside from the essentials like a computer and telephone, keep just a few meaningful things on your desk. When the surface and surroundings are clear, there's plenty of room for positive chi to flow!

Warm, soothing orange and its related spectrum of desert-like colors can be good for teamwork and collaboration. Use this color in any rooms where you are likely to meet with others to work toward common goals.

Stay away from dark tones on your ceiling. Keep it as white and bright as possible, since the ceiling represents higher aspirations. This is especially true for attic offices—you can't get any closer to your higher aspirations than in an attic home office.

SHED A LITTLE LIGHT

Light also affects the balance you have in your home office. Of course, natural light is the best to have in your workspace, so windows or full-spectrum light bulbs work best. Try to avoid using fluorescent lighting in your home office—such lighting inhibits creativity and has been known to create headaches and eyestrain. Use live plants to balance electrical energy in the room.

ELEMENTARY TIPS FOR HOME OFFICES

Your home-office workspace should be as pleasant and inspiring as you can afford to make it. You can achieve some measure of delight in your home office by looking at the five elements as they relate to your work and surroundings.

How you set up your home office largely depends on what kind of work will go on there, that is to say, with which of the five elements your work is associated. Feng shui employs the elements of wood, fire, earth, metal, and water in achieving balance, and each element is represented in a different bagua or section of the bagua.

For added balance to your home office, look for a nice mixture of elements that corresponds to the bagua (see Chapter 1) in each section of your room. For instance, a wind chime hung in your wealth sector works well with its corresponding image—wind. The center entrance to your home office is in your career sector, which has water as its element. So, putting a water fountain or something blue in the doorway is considered good feng shui placement.

Creative types such as writers and illustrators might want to include a tabletop fountain, or even an attractive blue bowl or glass of water, in their workspace since these can represent water. Creative pursuits require their practitioners to dig deep within themselves, while remaining quiet and contemplative on the surface.

Other elements are associated with other professions, such as:

- **Metal**—accounting and management. Use metal art, a trophy, or a metal desk.

- **Earth**—medicine and social work. A small granite or clay sculpture or pot can represent this element.

- **Wood**—marketing, selling, and teaching. Paneling, a wooden desk and chair, or picture frames are easy to incorporate into your office.

- **Fire**—sports and public relations. A candle or two is great, especially with a stimulating scent that keeps you alert. Alternately, you can use a soft, pleasing lamp or string of lights.

Incorporating the five elements in some way when you decorate and arrange your workspace can boost your productivity.

Chapter 11

Your Outdoor Spaces

Every year, people spend billions of dollars on vacation travel just to "get away from it all"— to go to that magical place where summers last forever and the beauty of nature has the effect of slowing down time. But, if you do it right, you can find peace, comfort, and rejuvenation in your own backyard.

Balance in Your Garden

———

In feng shui, a healthy garden means, quite simply, a healthy life. Untidy gardens with rampant flowers and weeds or foliage can drain the healthy chi that surrounds your house, not to mention your own personal chi on the day when you finally do find the time to tend the garden!

Remember, your garden's main purpose in feng shui is to soften the negative energy caused by the sharp edges directed at your house.

Always begin your garden work with a space clearing, which in this case means getting out your garden tools and removing any weeds or debris in your yard or garden area. Trimming the hedges that line your walkway can clear the path to good chi outside, and a clean sweep is also good for activating the chi in the earth.

Good balance and healthy chi in your garden are easy to achieve using the principles of yin and yang, the bagua, and the five elements. Add water and a good dose of intention, and you're all set to begin creating the garden escape of your dreams!

Adding the Elements to Your Garden

———

Before you can fully understand and apply the five elements of feng shui to your garden and the outside of your home, you need to take another look at the principles of yin and yang. Think about it, and take the time to look around; you'll be amazed at how many things in your garden are yin-yang. The garden is definitely one place where opposites attract!

EQUAL AND OPPOSITE

Achieve a yin-yang balance in your garden by combining unusual shapes, orientations, structures, or arrangements that contain different energies. For instance, flat land needs to be combined with undulating land (or rolling hills); stone (including pebbles, gravel, brick, or marble) should be combined with free-flowing water.

Combine nonliving objects (like angel statues or perhaps a birdbath) with living objects such as plants, animals, and birds. Animals in pairs enhance the power of two, which greatly helps your relationships. Aside from that important benefit, however, animals help to keep chi active both inside and outside your house.

Other areas of yin-yang balance in and around the garden include combinations of grassy spots with paved ones (as in lawn with driveway or walkway), and flowering plants (such as morning glories) with foliage plants (like pachysandra).

WITHSTAND THE ELEMENTS

Knowing how the five elements relate to each other in the creative and destructive cycles is critical to creating a harmonious, total garden experience. As a quick reminder, in the creative cycle, fire creates earth, earth creates metal, metal holds water, water nurtures wood, and wood feeds fire. In the destructive cycle, fire melts metal, metal cuts wood, wood moves earth, earth muddies water, and water puts out fire.

- **Wood** is organically represented by trees and plants but can be materially represented by adding a wooden deck, gazebo, patio furniture, or fencing. On the bagua, wood is connected to the areas of family/ancestors and helpful people, so wood elements ideally may remind you of your family "roots," or may actually be gifts from family either through inheritance or just plain giving.

- **Fire** can be represented in your garden by lighting (even torch lighting), candles, outdoor grills or clay firepots, crystals, sun symbols, and triangular shapes (including triangular-shaped plants such as pine trees, hostas, and astilbes). The bagua's fame section is home to the element of fire.

- **Metal** exists in many places surrounding your home, from the yard sprinkler to wind chimes and gazing balls. The shape associated with metal is round, so anything round in your garden counts toward use of the metal element. Wind chimes, of course, also activate the chi outside your house and have the protective bonus of letting you know when an intruder or a storm is near. Since metal is associated with the children and creativity section of the bagua, a metal swing set would also be appropriate in your backyard area.

- **Earth** exists all over your garden in obvious places (such as flower beds and grass), but it can also be represented by stone sculptures or terra-cotta planters, wind chimes, or garden stepping stones. Gravel, brick, and clay are also earth elements; use them to balance energy in your garden. The bagua position of the earth element falls in the marriage and relationships corner.

- **Water** should be in as many places as possible in your garden, since it is the element that creates wood, which feeds fire, which creates earth. Most often, water in the garden comes in the form of ponds, rivers, lakes, waterfalls, and birdbaths. A small wood and metal park bench overlooking a tiny pond in your backyard could be the perfect spot for meditation and quiet reflection. Do whatever feels right to you in terms of water placement; whether it be a pond or simply a reflective surface such as a mirror or a piece of glass, place it with intention. Whichever you choose, use it to reflect on your career, too, since this is the area of the bagua containing water as its element.

Be sure to include a place to sit so that you can always take time to stop and smell your roses. A park bench located in a special place (such as in the marriage corner of the bagua, near a small gazing pond) can add a meditative or calming aspect to that area of your life.

How you choose to use and symbolize the elements in your garden (or anywhere) does not have to follow set rules, as long as your intention is in keeping with your goals.

Using Colors Strategically

The significance of the bagua in the garden doesn't stop with the elements. It also includes the use of color in your peaceful retreat, and color, placed strategically and with good intentions, can have a healing, almost magical power.

MINDFUL PLANNING

How should you go about planting the seeds to sprout your best possible future? Look at the bagua and its nine areas of intention to determine which colors will be likely to harvest your best opportunities in life.

- **Career—Black.** Although this used to present a bit of a challenge to the novice gardener, today there are more choices than ever in this color category. Choose from chocolate cosmos, black-faced pansies, black irises, black Johnny jump-ups, black daylilies, and even black roses.

- **Knowledge—Blue.** Use blue flowers such as ageratum, morning glories, nigella, bluebells, bachelor's buttons, petunias, forget-me-nots, and hydrangeas.

- **Family—Green.** Restful shades of green in foliage like hostas, ferns, and shamrocks, or in herbs like parsley and dill will represent your family corner.

- **Wealth—Purple.** Plant larkspurs, purple ice, geraniums, pansies, asters, purple coneflowers, heliotropes, lavender, or violets to enhance your prosperity. You can also have African violets inside your house.

- **Fame—Red.** Achieve good representation of fame and recognition by using the color red in your garden. Draw fame to yourself—or at least enhance your reputation—by using this color in the fame area of your garden. Dahlias, sweet William flowers, cockscombs, petunias, zinnias, snapdragons, impatiens, California poppies, roses, and red trumpet vines work very well.

- **Relationships—Pink.** Pink is a soft, caring, and tender color that takes the edge off challenging relationships and keeps the tenderness in long-term ones. In the relationships corner of your bagua, you can plant pink roses, snapdragons, zinnias, dianthus, impatiens, geraniums, azaleas, and anemones, to name but a few. A rose by any other color simply won't do in the love corner!

- **Children/creativity—White.** Healthy shades of white will benefit the children and creative ideas corner of your garden. Moonflowers are wonderful in this area, as are petunias, alyssums, impatiens, pansies, lobelias, cleomes, foxgloves, irises, veronicas, peonies, Shasta daisies, and chrysanthemums.

- **Helpful people/travel—Gray.** Since it balances the yin-yang energy of black and white, harvest the helpers in your life by using the harmonic effects of gray. Or use it as a celebration of your own service to others. Plant lamb's ears, junipers, gray heucheras, silver-foliaged lavender, artemisias, and woolly thyme. If your intentions are to have this area as your travel corner, plant exotic flowers or foliage from other lands, like a Japanese maple.

- **Health—Yellow, brown, and orange.** Finally, enhance your own health or that of your family by planting the earthy shades in the center of your garden. Marigolds, zinnias, Mexican sunflowers, pansies, daylilies, cassia, butterfly weed, and chrysanthemums work nicely in the health section of your garden's bagua.

Plants and flowers carry special significance and meaning. For instance, the chrysanthemum symbolizes endurance and long life, juniper represents tolerance, hydrangeas signify achievement, and pine trees depict longevity. Every tree and every flower tells a story about how you see yourself— and they exist to support us in our environment. Honor their contribution to your well-being!

Because your choice of plants, and where you place them, is dependent on many factors, not the least of which is your green thumb, the ultimate decisions on how you choose to apply the principles of feng shui in your garden are entirely up to you.

NOBODY'S PERFECT

Nature, of course, is full of imperfection—so don't rush out and get one item of every element and every color to put in your garden. As with anything else in the Black Hat Sect of feng shui, you must ultimately go with what feels right to you. Which colors speak the most to you right now, at this point in your life? You may be attracted to a particular color, shape, or element because of a current life situation. You can always make changes later on, after one situation has passed and you are working through another!

Your preferences can also reflect the current energy of your house. If your house feels comfortable, your garden will likely exude the same characteristic—after all, it's all about you and where you are at this stage of your life.

The Shape of Your Garden

Ideally, your garden and yard form a perfect square. But many yards aren't like this, so what's a feng shui gardener to do?

If your yard happens to be triangular, you can plant some trees or bushes to cut off the sharp angles of the yard. This will also make your yard appear square. The area behind the trees or bushes can be a perfect spot for a meditation area, or even a rock or vegetable garden.

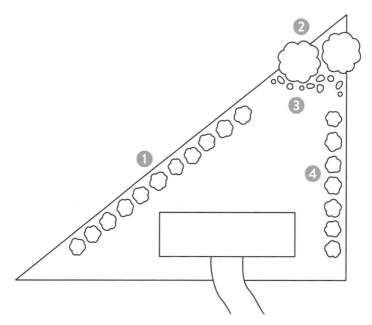

▲ An irregular yard can be made to look more square (the ideal shape) by planting a squarish rock garden (❸) and then filling in around it with shrubs or trees (❶, ❷, ❹).

LAND FORMATIONS

Ancient Chinese thinking speaks to the lay of the land itself. The Chinese believe it is best to have a mountain in the backyard and flowing water in the front. In traditional feng shui, the luckiest homes are those embraced by the four "celestial" animals: white tiger (west), green dragon (east), crimson phoenix (south), and black turtle (north). Combined, these animals offer the home-owner support, protection, wealth, and abundance in all things.

You should be able to see all four animals from inside your house, looking out. The higher dragon hills are usually to the left, lower tiger hills to the right. When the front of the house has a slight hill, this is said to be an auspicious crimson phoenix position. Turtle hills are always behind the house.

RIVER OF PROSPERITY

To incorporate the positive chi of water in the front yard, keep in mind that small ponds or even antique water troughs can do the job. You shouldn't have to build a moat! The Chinese believe that having water near the house is always a good thing, or *wang shan, wang shui* (which means "good for people, good for money"). The thinking is that what is good for the mountain is good for people, and what is good for water is good for money. Since water is a precious resource that is critical to all life, having some in your front yard will show the universe that you intend to always have enough resources at your disposal.

Birdbaths are a wonderful way to add the water element
to your garden and activate the positive chi of nature.
Remember that the activity of birds dipping
in the bath will spread lots of chi!

Less Is More

One of the nice things about visiting China is seeing the beautiful simplicity of its gardens. For the Chinese, less is always more. Chinese gardens accent simplicity and usually include one tree or bush, or focus on one type of flower at a time. There are not layers and layers full of impeccably landscaped floral arrangements!

Remember to clear garden clutter regularly—
prune, weed, clear, rake, and water on a weekly basis.
Overgrown gardens contain oppressive energy.

Here are some tips to keep your garden crisp and clean—the feng shui way:

- Alternate a succession of budding trees or flowers in bloom throughout your landscape. Plant evergreens in each corner of your garden's bagua to ground your success and cultivate your life's potential.

- Contain the chi in your garden by creating boundaries or borders with bushes and shrubbery. A fence would work too. Creating boundaries helps keep the chi contained in your immediate surroundings, not dissipating into thin air.

- Create a compost area in a place that feels right to you. Most people drop compost over the ledge of their backyard if there's a drop-off, but you can also incorporate a composting center, so to speak, in your wealth corner. Think about it: You are taking what has grown from the earth and provided for you, and returning it to the earth for another growth cycle. This is nature's prosperity center!

- Invite a sense of mystery and intrigue in your garden to keep it interesting. Add or change elements often, especially things like outdoor art or sculpture. Incorporate colorful objects of different shapes to maximize a sense of interest, wonder, and excitement in your garden.

- Finally, treat your yard with love and respect. Your landscape is a living thing that "talks" to you, your family, and just about everyone else who stops by for a visit.

Your garden and its surroundings communicate a message to others and create a particular feeling in those people too. How many times do you hear, "Wow, it is nice and peaceful here!" That's what others should be saying to you about your garden.

Outdoor Structures

Gardens can be self-contained spaces offering a plethora of organic pleasures, but they can also be home to small structures like greenhouses, sheds, or cottages.

Greenhouses come naturally equipped with their own light, so that's not an issue. But size and location are definitely important. A greenhouse should be in proportion to the landscape; it should never be so large as to overwhelm it, nor too small to perform its intended duty. Of course, a greenhouse should always be located near a water source.

Make your garden a peaceful, meditative retreat. Put in a small pond with a park bench next to it, or a gazebo with built-in seats. Garden stones and lighting balance out the elements, making your retreat a perfect yin-yang spot.

Sheds are perfect places to store outdoor furniture in the wintertime, or lawn accessories and tools in the summer. Just keep your shed in a good location several feet from your house—if it's too close, you'll worry about the yard work you haven't gotten to yet, but if it's too far away, well...out of sight, out of mind.

A small cottage, tiny home, or studio in your yard can be a wonderful escape from the rest of the world, a place for reading, journaling, meditating, or just plain relaxing. As with the shed, find a good location that's not too close by (you'll feel guilty when you're not able to relax) or too far away (it will always seem like you are struggling to break free from your regular routine).

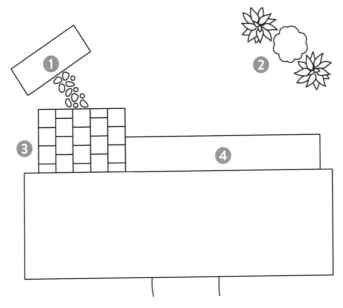

▲ A wooden shed (**1**) should stand alone and be balanced with shrubbery or flower beds (**2**) to add the natural chi of living plants. It can also be connected to your living spaces through natural elements like a rock path, a stone patio (**3**), and a wooden deck (**4**).

The choice of which kind of structure to include in your backyard is entirely yours; just be sure to position any poison arrows (sharp edges of the structure) away from your house so that you don't send any negative chi back toward your home. That would defeat the purpose of a peacefully intended freestanding structure.

Let's not forget the kids! They, too, can have an outdoor structure like a tree house or a playhouse, which will raise the levels of the fun "fire" element in your yard.

Cultivating Energy

Once you create a peaceful oasis in your garden, you'll want to connect your own personal energy to the space. The best way to do this is by incorporating what in feng shui are called the eight enhancements: light, color, sound, movement, life, straight lines, stillness, and mechanical devices.

LIGHT

Anyone who's ever embarked on an ambitious garden project, or who's read an edition of *The Old Farmer's Almanac*, knows that there is a time to plant and a time to grow. But there is also a place to plant for real garden success. Certain plants (and most flowers) do better when there is more light, while others (usually bushes and thicker foliage) do just fine when not in direct sunlight. Take the time to plot out the areas of your garden that receive more light so that you can plant your flora in a place where it will absorb the energy of the sun.

Keep in mind that light is one of the best ways to use the principles of yin-yang too. Sunlit areas should be next to shady ones, and brightly lit corners should be near areas left in darkness. Balancing light in the garden is tricky business but can be achieved with planning and forethought.

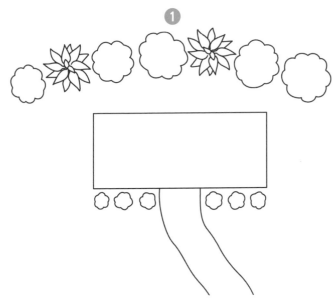

▲ If your backyard features a view of the neighbor's yard, plant foliage strategically as a positive boundary in place of (or in front of) a fence (❶).

COLOR AND SOUND

Remember that adding color emphasis to a particular area of your garden's bagua will focus more energy on that area of your life. If you want more fame and recognition, for example, use lots of red!

Nature is full of wonderful sounds, from trickling water to singing birds. The wind has a sound, if you are quiet enough to listen.

To attract more positive nature sounds, plant bamboo in your garden. It makes a very subtle sound as you brush past it.

MOVEMENT, LIFE, AND STILLNESS

Bird feeders work well to increase the movement of chi by birds and small animals. Squirrels can be good movers of chi! Pet animals can also be a positive source of chi activation in your yard or garden. Fishponds work as well.

Wind chimes certainly move chi when placed indoors, but they are especially good for enhancing a garden space. Antique water pumps will also represent a sense of flow and movement.

You may use your garden primarily for solitude and reflection. In Zen, quiet stillness is an essential ingredient for peaceful meditation. Sculptures, stones, and other permanent fixtures can be good focal points for meditation in your garden.

STRAIGHT LINES

In other areas of feng shui practice, straight lines are not considered good for chi, since they allow the chi to flow too quickly. As you have learned, curved lines are best. The exception to that concept is in gardens, where there are already too many curves. It's a yin-yang thing, but you can definitely employ a few straight lines to an otherwise meandering garden.

Feng Shui for Small Spaces

Creating the ultimate feng shui garden can be a wonderful experience, one rife with possibilities if you have lots of space to do all of the things you'd like. But what if your space is confined to smaller areas, as is the case with tiny homes, apartments, and town houses?

Even if you don't have oodles of space to plant every pachysandra or morning glory you'd like, you can still apply feng shui principles to keep a garden that flourishes on a smaller scale.

WAY UP IN THE SKY

For rooftop or balcony gardens, which many city dwellers tend from their high-rise apartments, apply the traditional Chinese garden rule of simplicity. Less will always be more in this space, and you'll want to keep all your possibilities open to the future by keeping your rooftop or balcony as open and simple as possible. After all, the higher rooms in your dwelling always symbolize your greater aspirations in life, and you don't want to dampen your dreams with too many living things requiring water!

Be sure to check for proper drainage from your garden. According to feng shui belief, rushing water will cause your finances and higher aspirations to roll right off your roof and into the street from the roof deck. Conversely, standing water represents stagnant chi.

If you have outdoor furniture in your rooftop garden, be sure that any small sitting areas are covered with a symbolic roof such as an umbrella or a small awning to protect you from catastrophes in life. Be extra mindful of the straight lines so apparent in most apartments, and balance them out with curved planters. Also, use window boxes with brightly colored flowers when you can, since they attract strong phoenix energy and can bring you prospects and helpful contacts. Remember to use bamboo as a tree alternative in an area that is too small to grow trees in. Bamboo has terrific luck energy!

DOWN TO EARTH

Lower-level or basement-type gardens need the same kind of attention, although here you'll be paying much more attention to light. If you don't get strong enough sunrays in this kind of garden, you might want to invest in some lighting especially tailored to greenhouses (and safe for outdoor use). This will help your plants flourish.

If you live in an apartment and cannot have an outside garden, create a small one indoors with a few houseplants, some quality lighting, and a small Zen rock garden or fountain nearby.

The difference between a flower and a weed is a judgment.
—ZEN SAYING

Remember that feng shui is about personal intention, and adapt its practices to your life and environment. Know that a small, simple garden will allow you to tend to a few things well, while keeping your potential for greater abundance wide open!

Outdoor Fun

With all the talk about the perfect elements, plants, directions, colors, and energies, it's easy to forget that your garden also needs to have some room in it for family fun. After all, what good is having a backyard if it's only a flower museum?

Designating the appropriate amounts of space for football, badminton, tree houses, swing sets (great movers of chi), and other fun activities will not only keep your family happily together during playtime, but will also add to the fire element of your feng shui landscape.

Balance in the garden represents the balance of nature.
Achieve it by contrasting textures, such as rough edges
of rock versus smooth water in ponds or fountains.
You should also be mindful of your garden's purpose:
to cultivate healthy bodies, both inside and out.

Always be sure to have another designated area for entertaining, since occasionally you'll want others to come into your garden for a sip of lemonade or a wine spritzer. Festive outdoor lights also add flair—and a fire element—to your outdoor parties and get-togethers.

A YEAR-ROUND RETREAT

The fun needn't stop when those autumn leaves start falling. For those of you who live in parts of the world where the climate changes seasonally, note that your garden is not just for you to enjoy in the spring and summertime. Each changing season brings with it a new chance for growth and positive change.

In the winter, look outside and appreciate the cycle of nature that is hidden beneath the frozen ground. In the fall, be thankful for the great beauty of the green season gone before, and be grateful for the harvest. Be mindful of each season and appreciate what each means in nature's cycle of change and renewal; don't forget that winter can be an excellent time for planning next year's garden surprises.

No matter when or how you do it, creating the feng shui landscape experience is a creative, or yin, activity, and it can reconnect you with missing or long-forgotten parts of your soul. In your feng shui garden, you and the earth join hands to surround your home with the best of all possible energies, empowering you to be a "life-giving" or chi-filled source of the natural resources needed to achieve your goals.

Connect with nature and you bring all of your feng shui efforts into full circle!

Glossary

As you continue reading about feng shui practices, you will also continue to learn about related topics, religions, philosophies, and traditions. The following terms are used (and defined) in varying detail in the text.

ancestors

In traditional Chinese culture, honoring ancestors is very important in maintaining the good health and prosperity of the family. Ancestors are represented in the family corner of the bagua, which is on the middle left side of the octagon.

bagua

An octagon that represents the nine intentions of your life. It is used as an energy road map that can help direct more positive energy to specific areas of your life. For instance, if you want to enhance your career, you could use the bagua to determine the career area of your home; you could then use the principles of feng shui to maximize your opportunities. In this sense, it can be a manifestation tool.

Black Hat Sect

The Black Hat Sect of feng shui relies heavily upon Zen principles.

Buddhism

A school of spiritual thought based on the teachings of the Buddha, who believed that we all possess the ability to reach a state of complete understanding of nature, our lives, and the universe. In Buddhism, enlightenment can be reached by releasing our earthly, mundane attachments in favor of higher spiritual thought. Much of feng shui (particularly in the Black Hat Sect) is based on the teachings of Buddhism.

career
The area of the bagua that represents your career. Located in the front center section of the bagua. Most people enter their homes in the career sector of the bagua. It is associated with the water element.

chi
Often called *qi*. The invisible life force, or life energy, that according to traditional Chinese culture moves about in and around our bodies and environments.

children
The area of the bagua that represents children and creativity. It is located in the middle right area of the bagua and is associated with the metal element.

Compass School
The Compass School of feng shui uses the compass to determine auspicious directions for energy. It is a highly intellectual versus intuitive school of feng shui thought.

creative cycle
In this cycle of the five elements, water nurtures wood, which feeds fire, which makes earth, which creates metal, which holds water. Each phase of the cycle enhances the next. Also called the productive cycle.

cure
When a negative position is encountered in feng shui, a cure can remedy the problem by reversing or redirecting the energy into a positive flow. For instance, if there is blocked chi in your doorway,

you can hang a crystal to get the energy moving. There are eight basic remedies in feng shui.

destructive cycle
Sometimes called the reductive cycle. It is used to reduce the power of a dominating element. Each phase of this cycle reduces or minimizes the next phase.

dragon
This animal of the Chinese zodiac represents eastern energy and the wood element.

earth
In feng shui, earth is one of the five elements that affect our lives. It is associated with relationships, resourcefulness, and earth colors.

eastern energy
This energy propels us into action.

fame
The area of the bagua that represents fame and reputation. It is located in the rear middle of the bagua and is associated with the fire element and the color red.

family
The area of the bagua that represents your family. It is located in the middle left side of the bagua and is associated with the colors blue and green.

feng shui
The traditional Chinese system of placement, harmony, and balance within the environment. The goal of feng shui is to achieve harmony with chi, or the universal life force. Literally translated, *feng shui* means "wind and water," symbolic of the movement of energy.

fire

Represents enlightenment and vision of self. One of the five elements, fire is associated with colors such as red and orange and with southern direction.

five elements

In feng shui, there are five elements: earth, wood, metal, water, and fire. These are symbolic of the seasons and have both creative and destructive cycles.

five senses

To achieve balance in feng shui, it is best to appeal to as many of your five senses (taste, touch, smell, sound, and sight) as possible in each room. Often, as we enhance a room's energy with wonderful items that appeal either to our visual sense, as with art, or to our sense of smell, as with potpourri, we forget that the other senses need attention as well. It is recommended to balance them in as many rooms as possible.

Form School

The primary school of feng shui thought, based on the ancient Chinese need to maximize the lay of the land. Much attention is paid to topography of the land in this school of feng shui.

health

The area of the bagua that represents the health of you and your family. It is located in the center of the bagua.

helpful people

The area of the bagua that represents the people who help you advance in your life. It is located in the front right area of the bagua. This is also commonly called the travel corner as well, and it is associated with heaven and the colors white, gray, and black.

house blessing

A ceremonial method of enhancing a space and endowing it with the strongest potential for good luck. It is usually performed after a space clearing.

I Ching

Ancient Chinese divination system, also known as the "Book of Changes." Much of feng shui theory is based on the *I Ching*.

intention

An aim that guides an action and gives it purpose and meaning.

knowledge

The area of the bagua that represents knowledge and self-growth. It is located in the front left side of the bagua. The colors associated with the knowledge corner include black, blue, and green.

luo pan

This is the name given to the feng shui compass used to determine proper flow or direction of energy in your home or surroundings.

marriage

The area of the bagua that represents marriage, partnerships, and important relationships. It is located in the rear right corner of the bagua. This is the corner where you'd most want pairs of things, to symbolize love and partnership. Associated colors are red, pink, and white.

metal

One of the five elements in feng shui. Metal represents structure and strength, but also creativity and recreation. Colors associated with the metal element include white, gold, and silver.

missing corner

An area of the bagua that is not represented by a room in your home. It's also referred to in feng shui as "absent space."

mouth of chi
In feng shui, the main entrance to your home is considered the "mouth" or opening of chi. It allows energy to come in from the front door and then directs chi through your home.

mudra
A series of symbolic postures and hand movements used in Hinduism to represent different stages along the path to enlightenment.

northern energy
In feng shui, energy from the north brings quiet, meditation, and stillness. Here, we can be introspective and nourish ourselves.

phoenix
A bird of great power, associated with southern energy and the fire element.

poison arrow
Any sharp corner or straight object from which chi is bounced at an angle. If you have such a situation inside or outside your home, a feng shui cure is recommended, since poison arrows are considered to be bad luck or negative energy.

qi
Another spelling of *chi*, which is the invisible energy or life force that is within us and all around us.

smudge stick
A tightly wrapped bundle of healing and spiritual herbs, used (with intention!) to clear or cleanse a space of negative energy.

southern energy
Changeable, unpredictable, and enlivening energy.

space clearing

In feng shui, a ceremonial method of removing negative energy in a room or structure and replacing it with a healthy flow of positive energy. This often involves walking through the structure with a smudge stick or lavender incense. A space clearing should be performed after any major change in the energy of a room (i.e., after an argument, redecorating, or remodeling).

Taoism

Sometimes called Daoism, this philosophy relies on intuition and the belief that we are one with nature.

tiger

Associated with western energy and the metal element. A "white tiger" is any tree, bush, building, fence, or landform located to the right of your home or business.

trigram

Most frequently associated with the *I Ching*, a trigram is a three-tiered set of broken and unbroken lines that symbolize the yin and yang that create all things and situations in life.

turtle

This animal in feng shui symbolizes the energy of the north and the water element.

water

Another of the five elements, water represents contemplation, reflection, and solitude. It is associated with blue, black, and the northern direction.

wealth

The area of the bagua that represents wealth and prosperity. Located in the rear left corner of the bagua. This is where you might position your desk if you have a home office, or where you would hang a crystal to activate wealth energy in your home. Coordinating colors include blue, purple, and bluish red.

western energy
Relaxing, creative yin energy.

wood
Represents growth, personal development, and the generation of new ideas or plans. Associated with green and the east. Wood is also one of the five elements.

yang
Creative, dynamic energy. It is often perceived as active and masculine energy. Yang and yin are complementary opposites.

yin
Receptive, feminine energy that is seen by many as passive and soft. Yin and yang are complementary opposites.

Zen
A movement of Buddhism that emphasizes enlightenment through meditation and intuition.

Index